D1456574

Six Weeks to a Better Level of TENNIS

by Dennis Ralston
with Barry Tarshis

Photographs by Phil Bath

Simon and Schuster · New York

Copyright © 1977 by Dennis Ralston and Barry Tarshis
All rights reserved
including the right of reproduction
in whole or in part in any form
Published by Simon and Schuster
A Division of Gulf & Western Corporation
Simon & Schuster Building
Rockefeller Center
1230 Avenue of the Americas
New York, New York 10020

Designed by Irving Perkins
Manufactured in the United States of America

1   2   3   4   5   6   7   8   9   10

Library of Congress Cataloging in Publication Data
Ralston, Dennis.
    Six weeks to a better level of tennis.
    1. Tennis.   I.   Tarshis, Barry, joint author.
II. Title.
GV995.R26   796.34'22   77-3289
ISBN 0-671-22580-4

*This book is dedicated
to all the members
of my family
and to all my friends
who have helped me
throughout my career
as a tennis player
and a tennis coach.*

Contents

Introduction

Collaborations between professional athletes and professional writers often tend to be patchwork enterprises, with the main concern of everyone—the athlete, the writer, and the editor at the publishing house—generally being that the book be published before the athlete's name has lost its celebrity value. *Six Weeks to a Better Level of Tennis* is, I'm happy to say, an exception. This is a book in which everyone involved —the athlete, Dennis Ralston; the writer, myself; and the editor, Peter Schwed—was motivated by the same concern: to produce an instruction book that met a need, that was well put together, and that did more than simply recycle a lot of old ideas that have been done to death in other books.

As the title indicates, the theme of *Six Weeks to a Better Level of Tennis* is improvement. More than an instruction book, it is a detailed guide on how to raise the level of your game, and it has been written primarily for that vast army of "intermediate" players who don't understand why they don't seem to get any better regardless of how much they play. Many people would argue that once an intermediate player reaches a certain level, it's virtually impossible to improve very much, but Dennis Ralston's contention, set forth in this book, is that you *can* and will improve, providing you go about it in the right way.

It's hard for me to think of anybody more qualified to help an intermediate tennis player raise the level of his game than Dennis Ralston. Ralston is that rare breed: an outstanding player *and* an outstanding coach. He was a successful tournament player while still in his teens, reaching the semifinals of Forest Hills when he was only seventeen. Ranked the Number One United States player for three consecutive years (1964–1966), he was forced to curtail his playing career prematurely, owing to chronic knee problems, so he then became one of the game's most astute and successful tennis coaches. Currently a World Team Tennis coach, he has coached four triumphant U.S. Davis Cup teams, and he was the captain and coach in 1972 when the U.S. Davis Cup team scored one of the most dramatic challenge round victories in the history of the Davis Cup, overcoming enormous pressure to defeat the Rumanian team at Bucharest. To a man, the winning United States squad credited Ralston for holding the team together.

Dennis, as most tennis people know, was ultimately relieved of his Davis Cup position in late 1975—a casualty of a complicated and unfortunate combination of events and personalities, the gist of which was Jimmy Connors's refusal to play for the U.S. Davis Cup team as long as Ralston was involved. Surrendering his Davis Cup position was a harsh blow for Dennis, who is genuinely patriotic, and who took great pride and satisfaction in his Davis Cup involvement, but he responded to the setback not with paranoia or self-pity, but with the determination to establish himself once again as a competitive tournament player. It is a measure of his resilience that in less than seven months after he made the decision to start playing again, he teamed with Rod Laver to win the doubles championship of one of the tour's most prestigious events, the United States Professional Indoor Championships, in Philadelphia. Two months later he coached the U.S. team to a convincing 5–2 victory over Australia in the annual Aetna World Cup in Hartford, Connecticut, and a year later was at the helm again as our team made an unprecedented sweep of the Aussies, 7–0—a victory that every member of the team credited in large part to Ralston's coaching.

Much of this book was written during the period in Dennis's life when he was dealing with the Davis Cup pressures and trying, at the same time, to get himself back into playing shape, but none of these pressures interfered in any way with his enthusiasm and interest in the book project. I saw him on numerous occasions during this period, and each encounter left me with a greater feeling of admiration, respect and fondness for the man. Tennis has far more than its share of insensitive, super-egotistical men and women, but Ralston is certainly not one of them. The image I held of Dennis prior to our initial meeting, was a very outdated one, based upon his temperamental outbursts as a teenage player; but I learned fast enough how misleading public images can be.

I ought to point out that the book took longer to complete than any of us had expected, not because we didn't work well together, but because each of us—Dennis, myself, and Peter Schwed—had our own ideas on how the material in the book could best be presented. Also, Dennis involved himself not only with the content of the book, but with honest, direct styling and text as well. "The idea is right," he must have said dozens of times as he went over the manuscript, "but it doesn't sound like me. Let's make it simpler, more direct." The last thing I expected when I began this project was to have a tennis player tell me how to write concisely; but I have to admit that Ralston's editorial judgment was right in virtually every instance.

A few acknowledgments are most certainly in order. Dennis's wife, Linda, had a large hand in the completion of the book, making a number of valuable suggestions after reading each draft. Mike Cardoza and Frank Craighill were instrumental in getting the project launched. Phil Bath took the sequence photos with his customary expertise and aplomb. Both Dennis and I owe special thanks, too, to Peter Schwed, who was patient enough to overlook our missed deadlines and enough of a tennis expert in his own right to add substantially to the book's content.

BARRY TARSHIS

Six Weeks to a Better Level of TENNIS

It goes without saying that most people playing tennis today would like to play it better. Yet a lot of players think that once you reach a certain level, or "plateau," with your game, it is almost impossible to get any better, regardless of what you do. Impossible, that is, unless you're prepared to quit your job, ignore your family and spend most of your time working away on a tennis court.

This view appears to prevail mainly among "B" club players, especially among players who didn't play tennis when they were younger, or else have never thought of themselves as being athletic. I'd like to have a nickel for every club player who's said to me: "I'll never get much better at tennis. I took it up too late"; or, "My problem in tennis is simply that I'm not a good athlete."

All right, maybe you did take up the game a little later than some people you know, and maybe you aren't the greatest athlete in the world. But are these necessarily the reasons you're not getting any better? I don't think so. I've been playing and teaching tennis for a long time, and I've yet to meet anybody who didn't have the potential to improve. Anybody.

Don't misunderstand. When I talk about improving, I'm not suggesting that everyone has the potential to become an "A" player, or that everyone's potential to improve is the same. Not everyone brings to tennis the same degree of God-given athleticism or the same ability to deal with the mental pressures of tennis. Not everyone has the same amount of time to play and to practice.

What every player *does* have, however, is the potential to improve in relation to himself. And I believe the reason most players do not improve in relation to themselves has little to do with when they took up the game or how athletic they are. It is more a matter of their not knowing how to go about improving. Just as there is a method for learning how to play tennis when a beginner, so is there a method for improving once you've reached a certain stage

1

Some Thoughts About Improvement

in your game. The basic purpose of this book is to explore this method.

DEVELOPING AN IMPROVEMENT STRATEGY

Some tennis players feel that the best way to improve is to go out and hit a lot of balls. Period. I don't agree. For some players and in some situations, this approach might produce improvement. But for most players, logging in hour after hour on the tennis court will not produce any truly noticeable improvement unless these hours are specifically designed for improvement.

To understand why this is so, let's explore the improvement phenomenon as it relates to tennis.

Tennis is fairly difficult for nearly everyone at first, but despite the difficulty, beginners tend to notice improvement in a short period of time. I've taught some beginners who were so impressed with their progress that they thought they were ready to play in tournaments after three lessons.

I'm not knocking this attitude. Confidence can carry you a long way in tennis. But these early gains can be highly deceptive and, in a way, dangerous. Dangerous in the sense that you may be lulled into thinking that the methods you started out with, and that brought you so far so quickly, are methods you can use successfully throughout your tennis career. Not quite. If anything, a lot of these methods can hold you back.

To illustrate what I mean, let's say you've never hit a tennis ball in your life, and the first day on which you come to me for a lesson, I tell you that the best way to hit a forehand is to first lift your front foot in the air and keep it

there while you're swinging. Let's not concern ourselves with *why* I tell you this. The important thing is that even with your foot suspended in the air, you're going to be hitting the ball better after two weeks than you did on the first day. In other words, you'll have improved.

But now let's look down the road a little bit. A year from now, when you start coming up against better players, sticking your foot in the air every time you go to hit a forehand is going to hurt your consistency, to say the least. Not until you make a fundamental change can you expect to improve beyond the early gains you've made.

I've cited a pretty extreme example, I admit, but I've done so to make a point. And the point is that the majority of intermediate players today are up against a problem similar to that which you would have if you were still trying to hit forehands with your foot in the air. It's an extreme example of what most intermediate players have buried into their strokes—built-in obstacles to improvement. There are certain things that you do with your strokes—or certain things that you don't do—which make it next to impossible for you to play tennis with any real degree of consistency. Until these things are corrected, your capacity to improve is going to be limited.

Now you may be saying, as club players have said to me many times, that once you develop a certain style of hitting the ball it's too late to change. I'll go along with this argument up to a point, but I don't think the argument has all that much to do with your improving. Not exactly, anyway. You can be hitting the ball in any number of different "styles" and still be hitting it properly, providing you're accomplishing certain things in the stroke, certain basic things that all good players accomplish regardless of their differences in style.

Most of the "certain things" I'm referring to are fairly obvious—or should be to anybody who's taken any lessons. Footwork, watching the ball, following through—there isn't a teaching professional who doesn't stress the importance of all of these. But the fundamentals that I stress more than any other, fall into three general categories. One is *early preparation:* getting into the proper "ready" position soon enough so that you don't have to rush your stroke. Another is *balance:* maintaining good body control at the beginning, during, and after you make contact with the ball. Finally, there is something that can best be described as *racket head movement,* which is nothing more, basically, than letting the racket head do most of the work in the swing —more so than the arm, shoulder or body.

The main reason I stress these three particular fundamentals more than any others is that if you've mastered them—if you're ready early enough, if you're balanced throughout your stroke, and if you're generating enough movement of the racket head—the other fundamentals tend to take care of themselves. On the other hand, if you're *not* getting ready early, and you're *not* balanced, and you're *not* getting enough racket movement into the swing, the other fundamentals really aren't going to do you much good.

My teaching philosophy in tennis is based on the idea that, if you can improve in these three areas, your strokes will become more solid and consistent and your overall game will improve noticeably. This is what I was getting at before when I said that everybody playing tennis today has the potential to improve. Whether or not you have the potential—or the time—to learn to hit the ball like an Arthur Ashe or a Chris Evert doesn't matter. You *do* have the potential to get prepared earlier, to improve your balance and to get more racket head movement into your strokes. These improvements, in turn, will help to make you a "better" tennis player.

MOVING BETTER

A basic aim of this book is to show you how to solidify your basic stroking technique. But it's not the only aim. There is a point in tennis beyond which technique alone cannot take you. Tennis is a game of movement. If there's one thing that more than anything else separates the average player from the good player, it's quickness—the ability to cover the court well, to get to the ball early.

Here, again, we're face-to-face with one of those areas in tennis in which a lot of people do not believe improvement is possible. "I just don't move well," I've heard many intermediates say over and over. "I'm not quick on my feet."

Again, I don't agree. True, some people are much quicker and more agile than others. Age, weight, athletic ability—all these things have a bearing on how quick you are on the tennis court. The important thing, though, is that you can improve on your quickness in the same way you can improve on your strokes. There are drills you can do. There are exercises—jumping rope, in particular—you can do. Above all, however, getting quicker on the court, as we'll see in a later chapter, is mainly a matter of *thinking quick,* of being alert, of forcing yourself to react sooner and to get into the habit of getting ready not when your opponent hits the ball, but as soon as you've hit it. The whole process is far more mental than most people think. Concentrate on quickness and you can improve upon it.

GETTING THE MOST OUT OF YOUR GAME

I don't want to minimize the importance of strategy as an element to good tennis, but I wonder if a book designed to help intermediates improve really calls for too much emphasis on the mental side of the game. I could sit for hours and talk about the best shots to use in certain situations and against certain types of players, but this advice won't take you very far it your game isn't technically sound, or if you can't move well.

This is true, to some extent, in pro tennis as well. Everybody in the pro game knows, for instance, that the best way to play Jimmy Connors is the way Arthur Ashe played him at Wimbledon in 1975, using a lot of off-speed shots and a lot of variety on the serve. The problem, though, is that not many players, even pro players, have the kind of variety that Arthur has. And Arthur would be the first person to admit that if he hadn't served well at Wimbledon, and he hadn't returned well enough to break Jimmy's serve, strategy or no, he would have lost.

The point here is that you have to be realistic. If you can't control the direction of your serve, it's silly to think about the *strategy* of serving. If you have trouble simply keeping the ball in play, it's foolish to worry about what sort of spin you put on your approach shots.

So, just as I do with technique, I'm going to focus on the *fundamentals* of strategy. And the one fundamental I'm going to stress more than any other is to keep the ball in play.

I know. Everybody says that. And no wonder. It wins matches. No matter what level of tennis you're talking about, it is the player—or the doubles team—who makes fewer errors who nearly always wins the match.

Stop beating yourself and you'll start winning more. The best way to stop beating yourself is to cut down on giveaway points; unforced errors.

Unless you're a machine, you can't totally eliminate errors from your game, but by disciplining yourself not to go for winners so often, you'll get more out of the game with better results.

Next to keeping the ball in play, the strategic fundamental I stress more than any other is to play within your own limitations. This doesn't mean that you don't try to improve weaknesses. What it means is you recognize that you're not Rod Laver, and you adopt a strategic approach that is realistically geared to your own strengths and weaknesses.

I remember a club tournament in which one player kept charging the net behind every serve and behind almost every ground stroke. This strategy might have made sense if this player had a good volley or a good overhead, but he had neither. So, he kept missing volleys getting passed with easy shots and lobs. He lost in straight sets. Someone asked him afterward why he persisted in this silly strategy. His answer was: "Well, I figured the only way I could win was to pressure him from the net."

Play within yourself. It's a simple rule but it's one of the most important rules of better tennis. This isn't to say that when openings present themselves you don't go for aggressive shots. But my experience with intermediate players has shown me that hitting winners is not the problem. The problem is that they make far too many unforced errors, errors that can frequently be explained by poor judgment; in short, trying to do too much with each shot.

GETTING TO KNOW YOURSELF

By now you should have some idea of how I intend to help you to improve your tennis. But I can't help you much unless you're willing to view yourself and your game with objectivity. Most players don't.

Example: You come to me for the first time, and inform me that the serve is the strongest part of your game. I take a look at it. Sure enough, you pound the ball almost as hard as Roscoe Tanner or Arthur Ashe, except for one little problem. You only get your first serve in one time out of five.

Example: You come to me and tell me how solid your ground strokes are and that you want to work on your net game. I have a look at your ground strokes. Sure enough, you do a pretty fair backhand imitation of Ken Rosewall, but only when you don't have to run a few steps to get to the ball. In those cases, you hit it out.

I'll never forget one woman player I worked with a couple of summers ago at a tennis camp for adults in New England. She had pretty good strokes, as long as I hit the ball right to her. The minute I hit the ball a little wide and she had to move, her game collapsed. She kept getting angrier with each miss until finally she said to me, "My pro at home always hits the ball right to me."

"Well," I said, "I don't think he's helping your game at all."

As I recall it, I didn't say it in a mean or sarcastic way. All I wanted to get across was the point that this woman was kidding herself if she thought that being able to hit balls that bounced next to her was the way tennis should be played.

"Well, I'll tell *you* something," she said. "*You're* not helping my game all that much, either," and with that she stormed off the court.

Admittedly, it's not so easy to get a clear picture of how well you play tennis. How good is "good?" How do you define strengths and weaknesses? By whose standards, and in relation to whom? Some players look like Wimbledon material when they warm up, but crumble the minute they have to make a shot under pressure. Other players look awkward when they warm up, but are tough as nails when it comes to a match: they know how to win.

My own definition of a "good" player is one who can play reasonably well against a lot of different types of players and under a lot of different conditions. This means that you're not going to come up to me after you've played badly in a match and say, "Well, the guy I lost to just pushes the ball. I can't play against a player like that. I need somebody who puts pace on the ball." And you're not going to say, "Well, it was windy out today, or too sunny, or it was Saturday morning, and I never play well on Saturday mornings."

The only way you can find out how strong your game really is, is to put it on the line against other strong players. I've run into many club players who have been number one in their particular circle for years. But then they go away on vacation somewhere and come up against a steadier, stronger player, and what happens? They lose.

Will they admit the other player was "better?" Not often. "I had an off day," I'll hear somebody explain. "I wasn't making shots." Baloney! The reason this player had an "off day" is probably that the other player was good enough to attack his weaknesses. He kept the pressure *on.* Too many players, including good ones, have a habit of blaming only themselves when they lose. I've found when you lose at tennis, the reason is usually that the other player played better.

Be honest with yourself. Unless you're willing to be objective about your game and willing to single out those areas that really need work, you're not going to improve. Self-analysis of your game alone won't do the trick, but it's the first step to the improvement process.

DO YOU REALLY WANT TO GET BETTER?

There is one more important point that I've yet to discuss regarding improvement. It concerns whether or not you're willing to make the commitment to improve.

I don't consider it my place to *sell* you on the idea of getting better at tennis. There are far more important things in life than being able to hit a tennis ball well, and I would be the last person to suggest that getting better at tennis is going to make your life any more meaningful.

But there are a great many people today for whom getting better *is* important. A while back I gave lessons to a man who'd been so successful in business that he was able to retire at the age of thirty-two. What was he doing with most of his time? He was playing tennis. Practicing. Taking lessons. Working as hard at his game as some professionals work, even though he knew that he could never hope to make his living playing the game.

Why was he committed to tennis?

Who knows? I'm not a psychologist, but I've met enough tennis "nuts" like this fellow to convince me that there are psychological factors at work here that are not at all easy to explain.

All of this is a roundabout way of saying that your reasons for wanting to get better at your game are your own affair.

I offer no magic formulas. I have an approach to improvement that I've seen work with just about all the intermediate players I've ever dealt with. It can work with you, providing you're willing to make a commitment to improve.

Commitment might seem like a heavy word for a book directed primarily to recreational players, but there's no use kidding ourselves. Without some sort of commitment on your part, you won't improve.

This commitment doesn't have to be as great as you might think. To improve at tennis you don't have to neglect other aspects of your life. The commitment I'm thinking about has to do mainly with the amount of tennis you're *already* playing—assuming, that is, that you're playing a minimum of, say, twice a week. If you can structure your present playing patterns so that a certain percentage of the tennis time you're already putting in is directed to specific improvement goals, you can do it. You can become a better tennis player!

The purpose of this book is to help you become a better tennis player in six weeks. I didn't say "good" tennis player, I said "better." You won't become a "good" tennis player until you've become better in a number of different areas. But you won't improve significantly in any area unless you set up a strategy specifically designed to produce improvement.

This is where the six-week program comes in. The basic idea is for you to set aside certain six-week periods throughout the year—as many or as few as you want—in which your principal focus is on improvement. In between these six-week periods, you can go back to your normal playing routine. But each time you do, you'll have improved to a degree that will make you a better player.

SETTING GOALS

The success of each individual six-week improvement program you undertake will depend largely on how intelligently and realistically you set your goals. The main thing is to be as specific as possible. It isn't enough to say "Over the next six weeks I'm going to work on improving my backhand." Improve it in what way, I would ask. Make it more consistent? More varied? Add more power to it? More depth? More top spin? The best and only realistic way to show a marked improvement of a stroke is to focus on one particular aspect of it.

The same principle holds true for any part of your game you're looking to improve. If you want to improve your serve, first figure out which aspect of your serve needs work. Do you want to cut down on double faults? Serve the ball harder? Put more spin in your second serve? Serve with more control of direction? Improvement in any of these areas will make your serve better, but the best way is to concentrate on one particular area during your six-week period.

I can't stress enough the importance of being as specific as you possibly can when you set up

2

Setting Up a Six-Week Program

your six-week goals. Setting up a six-week goal that is unreasonable will discourage you. It might even sour you on the whole business of getting better. Be realistic. Don't be in too much of a hurry. If, in the period of a single year, you can devote even as few as two or three six-week segments to certain parts of your game, within two or three years you'll have progressed far and away beyond the point you would have reached had you not taken the time to work on improvement in this manner.

SETTING PRIORITIES

Before you can start developing improvement goals, you need a general idea of what you're trying to accomplish overall with your game. A sense of priorities, in other words. Most players don't operate in this way; that's why so many of them have trouble improving. I've noticed players working on sophisticated shots like a top-spin lob when their games have much more fundamental weaknesses. Sure, a top-spin lob is a great stroke to have, but it's more important to be able to return serve well, or to have a second serve that doesn't always put you on the defensive.

A fundamental goal for every intermediate tennis player, to my mind, is the elimination of any obvious weaknesses. Weakness, of course, is a relative term. It means something different at each different level of the game. I would define weakness as any part of your game that gets you into continual trouble, whether it's a specific stroke, like the backhand volley, or whether it's a larger area of your game, like quickness or conditioning.

If you don't know where your weaknesses are,

it's time you started thinking about them. There are any number of different ways you can isolate weaknesses. A good way is to get a friend to watch you play and to take note of which shots you're missing consistently. You might find that you're having trouble with shots that land short on your backhand side, or wide forehands, or low volleys.

Another way is to go out and test yourself. Take the forehand, for instance. See how many times you can keep the ball in play consecutively when you're going crosscourt with it or when you're going down the line with it. Try the same thing on the backhand. Test your serve. See how many times in a row you can hit a good serve. I can remember one of my first teachers saying to me, "Once you can hit a shot twenty times in a row without a miss, then you can consider that shot a dependable part of your game." I'm not convinced that twenty is necessarily the magical number, and I have variations in the suggestions I make later on, but the basic idea of *consistency* is absolutely right.

The key phrase in this statement is "without a miss." A number of different tests have been suggested over the past few years to measure the technical proficiency of tennis players, but not enough of these tests take into consideration what, in my view, is the most important factor in hitting the ball—the ability to make the same shot over and over. Consistency.

If you are not sure where your strengths and weaknesses lie, I suggest you go through some of the tests included in the appendix (see page 101). These tests should help to isolate those parts of your game that need the most work. Once you've developed an idea of where your relative strengths and weaknesses lie, you can then tailor an improvement strategy geared to your particular needs.

THE SIX-WEEK PROGRAM

Once you've come up with an area of your game that you want to spend six weeks improving, you're ready to map out a definite improvement strategy. The actual mechanics of improvement can take on any number of forms, but in this book I'm going to be concentrating on four areas:

1. Watching—and learning from—better players
2. Solo drills
3. Rallying drills
4. Match play application

How to Improve by Watching Better Players

If you know what to look for, you can help your game considerably by watching good players. The trick is not to get too caught up in the match itself, but to focus in on certain things—things that relate to your own improvement needs.

What you fix your attention upon is mainly a matter of what you're trying to do with your own game. It's unrealistic, of course, to think that you can hit your backhand exactly as Arthur Ashe does, or hit your forehand exactly as John Newcombe, but you can still pick up a lot of little pointers by closely observing the stroking styles of these, or any top player, and by trying to keep a picture in your mind of how they hit the ball when you're practicing on your own strokes. When I'm having trouble with my own serve, for instance, I try to visualize Arthur Ashe's motion. Even though I really don't serve as Arthur does, it still helps.

The most convenient way of watching good players is to catch them on television, but there are limitations to television viewing. You can't control the camera shots or angles, and the commentary can sometimes be distracting. Better to go in person to a tournament. It's easier to do this today than it's ever been, now that there are so many tournaments. If you can, try to find out where the players are practicing. In many cities, the public can attend practice sessions free.

Don't overlook local tournaments. You can sometimes learn as much from watching two very good amateur players as you can from watching professionals, mainly because you should be able to identify more easily with the good amateurs. Here again, it's important to be selective in what you look for. Don't try to incorporate every successful idea into your own game. Stick with fundamentals, like early preparation and balance. Be observant and open, but be realistic as well.

Solo Drills

I include under solo drills anything you can do that can bring about improvement, on or off the court, *by yourself.* Some of my self-help suggestions you can do at home or at your office, with nothing more than a racket and a large mirror. There are any number of good drills you can do on your own on a tennis court. When Billie Jean King first took up the game, she used to spend hours just bouncing and hitting balls from one end of the court to the other. There are many of these solo on-court drills that can help improve certain areas of your game, although I recognize that many people find it impossible to get an empty court.

Rallying Drills

Practice drills are the meat and potatoes of most improvement strategies that are aimed at solidifying certain aspects of your stroking technique. The problem here, of course, is that to practice you need a cooperative partner, or else a ball machine. How you go out and locate a practice partner is something you'll have to figure out on your own, but once you find a cooperative partner, make sure you get the most out of your practice time. Don't just go out and hit balls around. Every time you go out to rally, go out with some specific goal in mind, something you're working on to improve. Ten minutes of concentrated practice, in which you're focusing on one aspect of your game, is far more advantageous than an hour of aimless hitting. If you're like most intermediate players, you don't have much surplus time for practice. That's all the more reason to make the best use out of whatever time you have.

One way to make practice time more interesting is to build in a competitive element. Play points, or games, with specific rules—rules designed to zero in on certain parts of your game. If you're looking to improve your volley, for example, you can structure the rules in a set so that the only way you can win a point is on the volley. Or, if your goal is to eliminate double faults, you might play a set in which each player is allowed only one serve. The possibilities are endless.

Match Play Situations

The true test of any improvement strategy is how well it holds up under match pressure. Under normal competitive conditions, a regular match is not the best arena for experimentation, but if your basic goal is to improve, the ground rules change. Let's say you've gotten into the habit over the past several years of running around your backhand whenever you can. I may suggest that for the next six weeks, in addition to other things you may be doing to better your backhand, you run around your *forehand*. You may lose. You may infuriate your doubles partner. Still, if you stick with it, your backhand will improve.

You have some flexibility when it comes to building an improvement strategy into match situations. If you want to work on your weaknesses but don't want to weaken yourself too much, you can pick certain times in a match—when you're well ahead in a game, or well behind—to experiment a little bit. Many professionals do this on occasion. When a top player gets comfortably ahead in a match, he may start to hit strokes you normally don't see him hit. What he's doing usually is practicing. Generally it doesn't affect the outcome, but once in a while, when you do this, your rhythm suffers, the other player starts to get better and, before you know it, you're staring at defeat.

I think it's worth the risk—certainly when your livelihood doesn't depend upon winning tennis matches. You can spend all the practice time in the world working on different parts of your game, but it won't do you much good until you put these newly developed skills to the test in a match situation. It's a matter of being prepared to lose some battles in the process of winning the war.

No improvement strategy can take you very far unless it's built upon a solid technical foundation. But every teaching pro has his own idea of how to develop this technical foundation and no two playing professionals hit the ball in exactly the same way; so one of the first things I had to do when I began teaching tennis, was to ready myself for students who might want to know why the methods I was teaching were not consistent with the way other pros had taught them or the way some of the best players in the game hit the ball. I don't ignore the differences between my approach and the hitting philosophies of other players and other pros. I emphasize that regardless of their individual hitting styles, all good players accomplish certain things when they hit the ball. Above all, they meet the ball in front and maintain good racket head control throughout the stroke.

If you can do these two things consistently— meet the ball in front and control the flow of racket—it doesn't matter which style or technique you use to hit the ball. But if you look into *why* good players are able to consistently meet the ball in front and maintain good racket control, certain common denominators become evident. I have already emphasized three of these common denominators in particular.

1. Early preparation
2. Balance
3. Racket head movement

Certainly there are other factors that affect the way you hit the ball. Positioning your body properly, the way you grip the racket, always keeping your eye on the ball—these things are obviously important, too. But I've found in working with intermediates, that if I can get them to improve in any or all of the three areas I've mentioned above, the other fundamentals tend to take care of themselves. So these are the areas I'll be coming back to time and again as we go through the basic strokes of tennis. Let's look at each of them a little more closely in order to see

3

Improving Your Basic Techniques in Six Weeks

how they affect your ability to control your strokes.

GETTING READY EARLY

How well or poorly you hit a ground stroke will usually depend on what you do before the ball arrives. Errors and miss-hits are most likely to occur when you are forced to rush your shot. And most of the time, the reason you have to rush the shot can be traced to one thing: a failure to get the racket back in time.

I've seen it hundreds of times. A player will anticipate a shot well, move to the ball smoothly, get his body turned and his feet positioned properly—do everything but the most important thing: get the racket back in time. Consequently, he has to yank the racket back and swipe at the ball. Instead of a smooth stroke, he gets a slap.

You should be ready to hit the ball *before* it bounces. Frequently, of course, you don't have the time and you have no choice but to hit the ball as best you can. But most of the time, you have more time than you think—*if you can concentrate on getting into a good hitting position as soon as possible.*

BALANCE

The basis of a sound stroking technique is balance. And for a good reason. Anytime your body is out of balance, your body's natural reaction is to restore the balance. There are mech-

anisms in your ears, in fact, whose main function is to help maintain equilibrium. These mechanisms aren't concerned with whether or not you're trying to hit a tennis ball, but they'll do their part if you do yours. Timing your stroke and controlling the flow of the racket becomes complicated if you're not well balanced, so make sure you are.

See why for yourself. Try bouncing a ball on the ground with your hand while you keep one leg in the air. It's tough. Now see how much easier it is when you're balanced. The same principle applies when you're hitting a tennis ball. It's the ability to hit from a well-balanced foundation—and the player who comes to mind right away is Ken Rosewall—that allows you the smoothness and fluidity that, in turn, produces control and consistency.

Little things can make a huge difference. All that extraneous movement so many of you incorporate into your strokes: the shoulder dipping down and then up on the backhand; the head ducking down on the volleys; the knees and elbows flying out in all directions on the serve. It's all unnecessary, and counterproductive. Extraneous movements increase the burden of those inner balance mechanisms I was talking about a moment ago. It's just another complexity for you to deal with that has nothing to do with hitting the ball!

Simplify your strokes! I make this suggestion time after time to intermediates who seem to think that the more little flourishes they can build into their strokes, the more power they're going to generate. It's just not true.

Look at Pancho Gonzales. Nobody ever hit a serve harder than Gonzales's but no player has had a simpler motion. There isn't a trace of wasted movement in Gonzales's serve. The power comes from a combination of balance, rhythm, fluidity, racket head movement, and the ability to hit the ball in the center of the racket. "If you have a nice, rhythmic swing," Gonzales used to say, "you don't have to hit the ball hard to get real power."

RACKET HEAD MOVEMENT

If I were pressed to name the one area of stroking technique in which the majority of intermediate players fall short, the area I would name would be racket head movement. Put simply, most intermediate players use too much arm and too much body in their swings. They work harder than they have to, and they do not permit the racket head to do what it was designed to do: provide most of the energy in the stroke.

To better appreciate the role of the racket head in the stroke, think for a moment about the technique of hammering a nail. When a young child hammers a nail, he generally keeps his wrist and arm rigid and the hammer head is little more than an extension of the arm. An experienced carpenter lets the hammer head swing much more freely and easier. The arc of the hammer head is, in itself, a source of energy.

It is no different in tennis—or, for that matter, in other sports like golf or baseball. The chief source of power in a stroke should be a racket head—not the arm and not the body.

ISOLATING ON THE WRIST

The crucial factor in racket head movement is the wrist. Racket head movement is generated by the wrist. The question is how much action is involved, and at what point in the stroke does the wrist come into play.

As with weight distribution, the role of the wrist in a tennis stroke is something I've thought about a great deal over the past several years. I've long felt that instructors who constantly emphasize the stiff wrist are not being helpful to their students. It's obvious that good players use more wrist movement than most tennis instructors recommend, and I don't go along with the familiar argument that only advanced players can generate wrist movement and still time the ball.

What happens, I'm convinced, is this: a player who isn't hitting the ball too well comes to a tennis instructor for help. This tennis instructor has been conditioned to look for the loose wrist as a reason for inconsistency. So the player hits a few balls and the pro immediately says, "Ah, yes. The wrist. Too loose. Your stroke is way too wristy."

This might be true. The player's stroke may well be a little too wristy. There is such a thing. But who's to say that the wrist is the main reason a player's having problems? I've usually found that when a player isn't stroking the ball well, the problem is much more fundamental: he's not getting ready quickly enough, or he's not balanced, or he's not watching the ball carefully enough. Assuming it is a problem at all, the wrist is generally a secondary problem.

I am not advocating a "wrist" or "slap at the ball" approach, and this will become clearer a little later in this chapter when we go through the basic forehand and backhand stroking motions step by step. What I'm saying here is that the only way to generate the amount of racket head movement you need in your strokes is to loosen up on the wrist—to let the wrist work naturally to allow the racket head to do most of the work on the stroke.

SOLIDIFYING YOUR GROUND STROKES

Now that we've gone over the fundamentals I'm going to be stressing time and time throughout this book, let's see how they apply to the two most basic strokes in tennis—the forehand and the backhand drive. The reason I deal with both of these strokes simultaneously is twofold: one, nearly all the basic technical elements are the same in both strokes; two, once you've reached the intermediate stage, you shouldn't have to differentiate between the two.

Before I go any further, however, let me talk briefly about grips. I don't concern myself with grips as much as other teaching professionals do —even when I'm working with beginners. I myself am a one-grip player—I use the Continental, a grip that is midway between an Eastern forehand and Eastern backhand—and this is the grip I teach to beginners. I recommend one grip only because it means one less thing to think about on the court, but I would not try to force my own thoughts about grips on any player. Mainly, it's a matter of personal preference. Some players, like Jimmy Connors, Harold Solomon and Björn Borg, use the so-called Western grip on the forehand, never mind that there are few, if any, teaching pros who would recommend the Western grip to beginners. I say, find the grip or grips that work best for you, grips with which you feel the most comfortable. If you can manage with one grip on both the forehand and backhand, fine. If not, try to work with as small a shift as possible between the two.

GETTING READY EARLY

The first step to hitting a good backhand or forehand takes place *not* when your opponent hits the ball, but as soon as you've finished your last shot. Very few beginners and surprisingly few intermediates seem to appreciate this fact.

Otherwise, you wouldn't see so many players hit the ball and then just stand there, with the racket dangling, as they watch to see where their ball is going to land. Watching to see where your own ball is going to land is one habit you cannot break too soon. All the watching in the world isn't going to have any effect on where your ball lands, but it *will* make a difference in the amount of time you have to get ready for your opponent's shot. As soon as you've hit a shot, you must immediately begin to think about the next shot. This means (1) moving into the correct court position (and we'll talk about court position in the next chapter) and (2) getting the racket ready.

In photo 1, I'm in the familiar "waiting" position, the position you want to get to as quickly as possible after you've hit your shot. Most of you have been taught the importance of this position, I'm sure, but I want to point out a couple of aspects of it whose importance you might not fully recognize. First of all, I am not all tensed up the way some players get when they're in the "waiting" position. I'm alert but I'm also relaxed. I have a comfortable grip on the racket, but it's not a white-knuckle grip.

Dennis in Waiting Position　　　**1**

Dennis in Ready Position Forehand and Backhand 2 3

Being relaxed plays an enormously important part in hitting a smooth stroke. If you're not relaxed before you hit the ball, you're not going to be relaxed while you're hitting it.

Secondly, when I am in the "waiting" position, my body is evenly balanced. Some players like to lean forward when they're in the waiting position, but I don't recommend it. The more balanced you are, the smoother your movements are going to be and the easier it will be for you to be prepared early.

GETTING THE RACKET BACK

Photos 2 and 3 show me in the "ready" position—the position you should ideally be in as the ball is bouncing. Getting to this position from the "waiting" position involves two things: one, getting the body turned; and two, getting the racket back. I'm not going to talk much about how you turn your body or the sequence of steps you take in order to line up your feet properly. I don't see the point of the carefully choreographed footwork sequences some teaching pros advocate. The key to getting your feet positioned properly is in getting your feet moving quickly and lightly, almost like a ballet dancer. If you're quick and light enough on your feet, you can get into position any number of different ways.

The backswing is a different story. There are basically two types of backswings. One is a looped backswing, like the backswing that Billie

Jean King likes to use on her forehand. The other is a more or less straight-back backswing, like the backswing John Newcombe uses. Players who use the looped backswing say that it helps them to time the shot better, and enables them to hit their shots with extra top spin. I prefer—and teach—as modest a loop as you can live with because my basic philosophy about hitting the ball is that the simpler you make the stroke, the better. The point, though, isn't so much *how* you get the racket back, but that you do it early enough and smoothly.

One tip I can offer to help you get the racket into the proper "ready" position early enough is to loosen up a little on your wrist, and let your free hand—the hand that's cradling the racket—start the racket moving in the proper direction. What you want to avoid is a tendency to move the elbow first, or lift the elbow too high, or get your entire body involved. Lifting the elbow too much on the backswing is a common mistake intermediates make on the backhand. It helps explain why so many players poke at the backhand instead of stroking it. With the elbow up and in front of your body, you have no option but to meet the ball with a short pokey stroke.

Another important consideration on the backswing is to keep it smooth. Don't just take the racket back by snapping the wrist back. As long as you have an idea—a "feel"—for where you want the racket to go, and as long as you allow your arm and wrist to be relaxed, a little push or a little pull on the part of that free hand will start the racket head back.

In any case, when I am back in this "ready" position, I am relaxed and I am balanced. Just as I was in the "waiting" position, I have a com-

Dennis Low 4

fortable grip on the racket but I'm not holding it too tightly. My elbow is straight out and not jammed into my side. It's comfortable and natural. If you were to give the racket a shove, my arm would move easily to either side. The racket head, meanwhile, is more or less on the same plane as my wrist and is pointing to the back fence.

In photo 4, I'm preparing for a ball that's bouncing low. Notice how I've bent my knees so that my body is more or less in line with the ball. This is very important. It is at this early stage of the swing that many intermediates get themselves into trouble. Too many players, when they see the ball is going to bounce low, bend over, as if they were picking up a dollar on the street. Bending over takes you out of balance. In photo 4, I'm still balanced. My racket has remained in the same relationship to my body that it was when I was standing in the upright position.

BALANCE AND WEIGHT TRANSFER

The key to balance lies in weight distribution —how the weight shifts through the course of the stroke. Somewhere along the line—and I don't know where or how—the idea spread that the best way to hit a tennis ball is to step into the shot and then swing, and to make darn sure in the process that you don't loosen up the wrist.

I don't know how this idea became such an ingrained part of our tennis teaching tradition. If good players "stepped and hit" every time they stroked the ball I could understand why so many pros teach this method. But good players *don't* hit the ball this way. And no wonder. The method defies basic logic.

Think about it a moment. If you are stepping into the ball before you make contact, you are, in effect, charging the ball. You might be able to hit the ball pretty well now and then this way, but it's difficult to hit the ball consistently well with a step-and-hit style. The problem is that by stepping into the ball, you frequently move your weight into the ball *too soon* so that you're making contact after your weight has gone forward. Usually, when you do this, you have no choice but to hit the ball when it's behind you, and when you're no longer in a well-balanced position. Committing the weight too soon also causes you to swing the front shoulder around (if you didn't, you'd probably fall forward)—that is, you open up the upper part of your body too soon. When you do this, you're fighting the ball again. On the one hand, you're trying to keep the ball on the strings for as long as you can and trying to extend the follow-through as smoothly as possible. On the other hand, by turning the shoulders, you are forcing the racket head to come off the strings too soon (this is what teaching professionals mean when they say "You're coming *off* the ball too early"). You lose control and pace, and you're forced to aim or steer the ball.

You can find out for yourself whether you're making this common error. Get hold of a racket and assume the forehand "ready" position. Take a few practice swings at normal speed. Now do it a couple more times in slow motion. As you go through the slow-motion part, pay attention to where your weight is in relation to the racket head. The best way to do this is to note the position of the racket head *as soon as you begin to feel* the pressure building on the front foot.

If the pressure is there before the racket head has reached the point where you ideally want to meet the ball—about six inches or so in front of the front hip—it means that during the most critical part of the swing, your weight has already moved forward.

Ideally, you should be making contact at the precise moment that your weight is moving from the back foot into the front foot, but so many players move their weight forward prematurely that I frequently recommend to a player that he or she try to be conscious of letting the weight flow *behind* the racket head a little. In other words, let the racket head lead the weight flow, and not vice versa.

GETTING THE RACKET HEAD INTO THE ACT

I hope I've been able to make myself clear up to now, because from this point on, for a while, my technique gets a little more complicated. It wouldn't be a problem if we were on a court together. I would simply guide you through the motions until you developed enough of a feel for what I'm getting at to practice it on your own.

There's no reason, though, why I can't communicate the same ideas here, provided you will go step by step with me. Our goal is to simplify

5 ⟫→

6 ⟫→

7 ⟫→

Sequence of Close-ups of Wrist in Dennis's Forehand Swing.

14

←⟪ **15**

←⟪ **16**

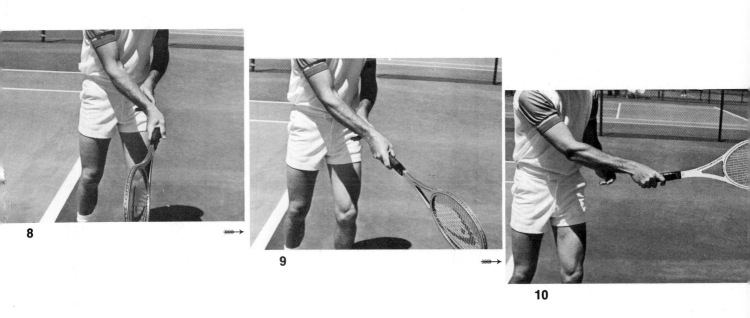

8

9

10

13

12

11

Sequence of Close-ups of Wrist in Dennis's Backhand Swing.

your stroke, increase both your control and your power by doing one thing: letting your racket head do more of the work in the stroke.

Let's start with the forehand ready position (photo 2, page 29). This time I want you to hold the racket as loosely as you can manage without dropping it. Notice how free the racket head swings when you hold it in this way.

Now, using mostly the fingers of your hitting hand to control the racket, let your hand move loosely back and forth. Don't worry if the racket head drops down a little. Just try to get the racket head moving in as easy an arc as possible.

Once you get a feel for that loose, easy racket head motion, you can grip the racket the way you normally do. But keep the wrist flexible. Not floppy loose, just flexible. Repeat the same back-and-forth motion you were doing a moment ago, allowing the racket head to sway easily back and forth.

Believe it or not, you're halfway home. Now all we have to do is to show you how to incorporate some of this free and easy movement into your swing.

Let's get to the heart of the matter: the how and the when of wrist movement.

I've tried several different approaches to this question over the past several years. The one that has produced the most successful results goes something like this:

First, you start the stroke with the wrist laid comfortably back, the way it is in the first of the sequence photos on pages 32–33.

As you're making contact with the ball, the wrist does not lock. Instead, let it continue its natural movement forward. The arm moves forward, too, so as to keep the ball on the strings

for as long as possible. There is no need to turn the wrist over, even though some of the pros, like Rod Laver, will roll the wrist a little in order to generate more top spin. Let the wrist complete its rotation naturally. Let the racket head flow forward naturally so that the follow-through almost takes care of itself.

Some players, myself included, swing the racket clear around to the other side of the body on the follow-through. This is okay as long as the strings stay with the ball for a long enough time, for that is what gives you control—keeping the ball on the strings as long as possible. The reason I like to see intermediates follow a stroke through with the racket out and up is that this pretty much forces them to stay *with* the stroke instead of pulling off too soon.

GOING THROUGH IT AGAIN

I don't expect you to be able to incorporate these elements of balance and racket head movement into your strokes overnight. It's going to take time, and I recommend a gradual approach. Here's a brief summary of what I've just gone over as far as the fundamentals of ground strokes are concerned.

1. *Get into the waiting position as quickly as possible.*
Keep the backswing smooth and direct, the wrist flexible and the grip comfortable, not too tight. Be smooth and relaxed. Make sure you're balanced. The racket should be well back, especially on the backhand side, but not so far back that you're straining. A good checkpoint on the backhand is to make sure the hitting hand is about even with the back hip.

2. *Don't commit your weight too soon on the stroke.* Let the racket head carry your weight along with it, and not vice versa. Start from a well-balanced stance. Avoid stepping into the ball or "throwing" your weight into the ball. Concentrate on smoothness and rhythm.

17

Dennis in Forehand Follow-through and Backhand Follow-through.

18

Forehand Sequence.

19

20

21

30

29

28

22

23

24

27

26

25

Backhand Sequence.

3. *Let the wrist generate racket head movement.* Start your wrist rotation as your body weight is moving forward. Don't slap at the ball and don't lock the wrist on contact. On both the forehand and backhand side, let the wrist move forward naturally.

SIX WEEKS TO A BETTER GROUND-STROKE TECHNIQUE

A six-week improvement program designed to improve your ground-stroke technique should focus on the three fundamentals I've just finished talking about: early preparation, balance, and racket head movement. The drills I suggest can be applied to either the forehand or the backhand, but if you need work on both, I recommend that you concentrate on either one side or the other in separate six-week periods.

Watching Better Players

You can pick just about any of the top players and, by watching them, get a lesson in the importance of ground-stroke fundamentals. Notice racket control before the swing—how the racket gets back early and to the same place every time. Watch their footwork—particularly Chris Evert's and Rod Laver's. If you can get a chance to see John Newcombe, watch how simple and direct he is on his forehand. He proves that you don't have to generate a lot of arm and body movement to hit the ball with power.

Focus on balance. Watch someone like Ilie Nastase. Nastase has great body control: he's hardly ever off balance when he hits the ball.

On the backhand side, you couldn't find a better example to follow than Ken Rosewall. Watch how quickly he prepares for the shot.

Another good thing to watch for when you're looking at good players is what they do wrong that causes them to miss. If you can figure out what a player did wrong when he missed a shot, then you can certainly begin to analyze what's wrong with your own game.

Solo Drills

EARLY PREPARATION. Practice moving from the waiting position to the ready position for at least a few moments every day—in front of a mirror, if possible. Try to get a sense of how the racket "feels" when it's in the "ready" position on both the forehand and backhand side. Work on the backswing, making it quick but smooth, keeping the wrist flexible and letting the free hand do most of the work.

BALANCE. Spend a few minutes, whenever you can manage the time, developing a basic forehand or backhand swing in which your weight is moving smoothly and is not preceding the swing. You can start by swinging the racket with the weight on the back foot and then working your weight into the stroke until you feel your racket head and body weight moving together (photo 29). Practice the swing with your eyes closed to get a better sense of weight transfer (photo 30). Simulate hitting balls at different heights, remembering to move the body as a unit instead of dipping a shoulder or dropping the racket head. Stay relaxed.

RACKET HEAD MOVEMENT. If you can arrange for some court time on your own, get a basket of balls and practice hitting either forehands or backhands on one bounce, with special attention to racket head movement. Try to hit the ball in the manner described on page 38, letting the wrist generate racket head movement but keeping the swing smooth throughout. You should be able to tell when you're generating racket head movement by the way the ball sounds when it hits the racket and by the additional pace the ball will have—with less body and arm effort on your part—when you hit it.

Practice Drills

EARLY PREPARATION.   Rally from the baseline and concentrate, in particular, on two things: (1) getting your body and the racket into the waiting position as soon as you've finished your stroke; (2) getting your body and the racket back to the "ready" position as soon as the ball leaves your opponent's racket. Keep doing it until it feels natural.

BALANCE.   As you rally from the baseline, pay close attention to your balance before, after, and during your swing.

If you feel your weight moving too far in front, keep your free hand lightly on your front shoulder to keep that shoulder from turning too soon. Since moving the weight in front too soon is such a common problem, I suggest you concentrate at first on keeping your weight a little behind the stroke in order to help you break the habit.

RACKET HEAD MOVEMENT.   Using the principles of early preparation and balance I've already described, try to get more racket head flow into your strokes. To do this, you must loosen up a little on the wrist, as described on page 34. Keep the swing smooth and relaxed. Don't break your wrist too soon. Don't slap at the ball. Relax. Ease up a little on the wrist and you'll find you don't have to swing quite so hard in order to generate power.

Match Play Application

Make up your mind that for the next six weeks, whenever you play a match, you are going to work on either your forehand or backhand, with special emphasis on the basic techniques we've been dealing with up to now. Forget your net game for the time being, and stop worrying about winners. Strive for basic consistency while incorporating elements of early racket prepara-

tion, good balance and racket movement into your strokes. If you're working on your forehand, try to make as many shots off that side as possible, even if it means running around your backhand. For the backhand, work the same strategy but in reverse. Make it a point when you're warming up to focus on these particular areas. Get the racket back early. Stay balanced. Loosen up on the wrist to get more racket movement into the stroke. Even if you make additional errors, try to stay relaxed. Remember, that making progress takes time.

IMPROVING YOUR VOLLEYS

Most of the common mistakes that intermediates make on ground strokes show up on volleys as well. The biggest problem is that most players muscle the ball too much. It's the same old story: too much arm, not enough racket.

Two characteristics of the volley go a long way toward dictating the best way to hit one. The first is that you rarely have as much time to prepare for a volley as you do for a ground stroke. The second is that you don't have to do much with the ball to get it to go where you want it to go.

I disagree entirely with instructors who advocate the "step and hit" method of hitting volleys. I don't even stress so much as other instructors do the idea of getting your body turned sideways. The most important thing to remember about the volley is to meet the ball in front of your body with a short precise swing and with a slightly open racket face. There's no need to make things any more difficult than that.

Breaking Down the Stroke

The basics of the volley break down into the following areas:

COURT POSITION. *Where* you happen to be on the court is a crucial factor in your ability to execute good volleys. It's tough to hit forcing or angled volleys when you're at the service line or in your own backcourt. Too many times, you're forced to volley shots off your shoe tops. Many players are not quick enough to move in any closer than the service line behind a serve or an approach shot. If you're one of these players, you shouldn't try to do too much with this first volley. Better to stroke it safely as deep as you can and then move in closer for the second volley— the one that will, with any luck, end the point. Don't make the mistake of crowding the net *too* much, however. If you do so, you're going to be vulnerable to any sort of a decent lob.

Your position on the volley will depend, of course, on the sort of approach shot you've hit: how hard and deep you've hit it, and whether you've hit it crosscourt, down the line or down the center. Most coaches will tell you to more or less follow the line of your shot—that is, if you're hitting down the center, straddle the service line; and if you're hitting to either side of the court, shade over toward whichever side of the court the ball has gone into. The idea behind this theory of position is that you can cover, in a step or two, all but the most difficult and expertly placed passing shots.

I recommend, though, that you stay close to the center of the court regardless of where the approach shot has gone (in singles, that is), because most players can pass you better cross-court than down the line. Besides, frequently, all you have to do on a down-the-line passing shot is block the ball back crosscourt for a winner. If you simply block back a crosscourt passing shot you're usually hitting the ball right back to your opponent, and you're setting yourself up to be passed more easily on the next return. So, even though theoretically you may be giving your opponent more open court to hit into on the down-the-line passing shot, you're still better off, I feel, if you concentrate on protecting the crosscourt angle by remaining in your own center-court position. If you've established position there, you can hit a good volley off to whichever spot your opponent has left most open.

BODY POSITION. I don't worry too much about body position on the volley. If you have the time, it's good to get the left shoulder turned toward the net, and to pivot to the right on the ball of your left foot (the reverse for lefties). Otherwise the main thing to bear in mind on the body position is to *stay balanced throughout the stroke.*

The position of the racket in the ready position is crucial on the volley. Most players take the racket back too far. You need not take the racket any farther back than the shoulder. Most volleys should be hit about chest or waist high. This means you can—and should—keep the racket level, the wrist comfortably laid back.

MEETING THE BALL. The actual volley stroke is a short smooth swing, with power and control coming from a combination of timing and racket head movement. The wrist does much of the work. Let the fingers start the racket moving. Then, as the racket starts moving forward, the wrist should begin to rotate forward, firming up on contact. Once you've mastered the timing, try to hit volleys with the racket face slightly open. An open racket face will generate the underspin that will help keep the ball in the court.

The volley is *not* a slapping motion. It's a shorter version of a typical ground stroke swing. Focus in particular on stopping the follow-through almost as soon as you've made contact.

Dennis in Waiting Position for Forehand and Backhand Volley.   31

Dennis in Ready Position.   32

TRACKING THE VOLLEY. Naturally, you have to watch the ball as carefully on the volley as you do on every other stroke in tennis. But it wasn't until a year or so ago, when I was working on an instructional film with a friend named Bud Freeman, a filmmaker, that I began to appreciate some of the subtleties involved in watching the ball—especially on volleys. Bud has filmed several sports and has focused in particular on the eye movements of athletes. One of the things he found out about me was that I tended to track the ball much like a baseball hitter at the plate, moving my eyes but not my head.

I had never been especially aware of whether I was moving my head or not, but after my conversation with Bud, I started to watch some of the better players, and what I saw confirmed Bud's observation. Among the better players, you see less head movement. Good players let their eyes do the tracking more than their heads.

It's hard to say how much better you'll start hitting the ball if you can train yourself to move your head less, but I had one experience that opened my eyes to what proper tracking can accomplish. I was working with a fairly coordinated club player who was consistently mistiming his volleys. He was getting them over the net, but wasn't hitting the ball crisply. Out of exasperation, I suggested that he hold one hand on his head to keep it still. He then proceeded to hit five of the best volleys of his life.

But don't interpret this advice too literally. When I tell you to watch the ball more with your eyes than with your head, I don't want you to stiffen up your neck. You have to stay relaxed. Keep your head as still as possible without being too rigid. What we're trying to eliminate are

**Sequence Volley—
Forehand.**

33

34

43

42

41

35

36

37

Sequence Volley—
Backhand.

40

39

38

those movements that cause you to mistime the stroke.

There is one other related point I'd like to make. When you're at the net, and the ball is coming at you, try to follow the flight of the ball without focusing in on the ball only. In other words, try to keep as much of the background in view without, of course, taking your eye off the ball. Keeping the background in view helps you to time your stroke better and hit your volleys more cleanly.

IMPROVING YOUR VOLLEYING TECHNIQUE IN SIX WEEKS

Improving your basic volleying technique (forehand or backhand) involves essentially the same process as improving ground stroke technique. Mainly, it's a matter of incorporating some of the specific points we've just gone over. The key points are (1) keeping your weight back until the swing; (2) keeping the swing as simple as possible, with the wrist providing the impetus for racket head movement; (3) seeing as much of the court as you can instead of zeroing in on the ball, and tracking the ball with your eyes instead of moving your head.

Watching Better Players

The main things to look for when you're watching the pros volley are court position, racket preparation, balance, and economy of motion in the swing. Observe good players closely when they're practicing volleys during the warm-up. Notice how short and compact a swing most of

them have. Rosewall, for example, has a very brief, almost delicate swing, and yet has one of the best volleys in the game. It's his timing and his balance that get the job done. Marty Riessen is a good player to watch because he's such a steady volleyer. He doesn't make the mistake of overhitting, and he places the shot very well. Among the women players, Billie Jean King is especially good to watch on the backhand volley; she meets the ball well in front.

The best place to see good volleying is in top-grade doubles matches. Watch how the better players get the racket ready early, even before they've moved into a position. Watch, too, how little it takes in the way of a swing to hit the ball cleanly and well—especially when the ball is coming over the net very fast.

Solo Drills

SHADOW STROKING. Set aside some time as often as you can to get accustomed to a simpler, more economical volley swing. Use your regular grip (I use and recommend the Continental grip), assume the preparatory volleying position, and go through the stroking sequence on either side you're working on, forehand or backhand. Make an effort each time to execute a smooth, short swing. Pivot the shoulders slightly but don't worry too much about the footwork.

Use your free hand either to push or pull the racket back. Don't take it any farther back than your shoulder. The key to the swing, remember, is to let the racket head, not the arm, go out and meet the ball. Don't slap at the ball. Keep the wrist laid back just before the imaginary contact point. Rotate it forward and firm it up again. Watch your balance. Keep your balance on the back foot. Minimize head movement.

Rallying Drills

BALANCE. Working with a practice partner or a ball machine, assume the proper volleying position (a few feet inside the service line, and straddling the center line between the service boxes). Concentrate on either your forehand or backhand volley at one time—don't alternate. Start with balls hit fairly close to you, at medium pace. Practice meeting balls with your weight slightly back. Minimize body movement and weight transfer.

RACKET HEAD MOVEMENT. Practice the technique described on page 27 to help get the racket head more involved in the volley stroke. Keep the stroke short and simple, letting the racket head go out to meet the ball, contacting the ball with the racket head slightly open.

TRACKING THE BALL. Hit volleys from the volleying position from either forehand or backhand, keeping as much of the background in view as possible. Let your eyes, more than your head, follow the flight of the ball to the racket. Try it both ways: first zeroing in on the ball, and then keeping the background in view, to appreciate the difference. Once you've become accustomed to this new way of "seeing" the ball, incorporate this technique with other basic volleying techniques already gone over.

Game Drill

Play sets in which no point can be won unless it is won off a volley. The volley can either produce a winner, or be the shot that precedes an error. The purpose of a game with these rules, obviously, is to force you to come to net more often.

Match Play Application

Hitting good volleys under match conditions is very much a matter of mental attitude. The shot itself is not technically difficult. What's difficult is making sure you're in a good position to hit the stroke. This ability relates to something we'll be talking about a little later: approach shots. For now, until you've mastered the basic volleying technique, come to the net as much as you can, even though your approach shots

may not be strong. Don't try to put every volley away. Hit them solidly and try to hit them deep enough so that they land beyond the service line. Be aggressive but don't be overanxious. You may feel you don't have a lot of time to volley a hard hit ball, but you probably have more time than you think—providing your swing is short and sweet.

IMPROVING YOUR SERVE

The serve is the one stroke you can't afford to be weak in if you hope to move up to more advanced levels of tennis. You can work around other weaknesses, but there's no way you can protect a poor serve.

The serve, however, is the easiest stroke to develop. It's one stroke you can conveniently practice on your own. Before you can get much out of such practice, though, you have to use the right techniques, and many intermediates don't.

The serving technique I recommend to most players who come to me for lessons is the one that Pancho Gonzales showed me when I was a teenager. Gonzales had what I consider the greatest serve of all time. It was the heart of his game, and it rarely deserted him. Yet, it was a very simple and natural stroke—much simpler, for instance, than the serving motion of John Newcombe or Roscoe Tanner or some of the other big servers on the circuit today. "Once the ball is up there where it's supposed to be," Gonzales used to say, "it's just like hammering a nail."

That simple?

Yes, that simple—providing you master a few basic points, the most basic of which is racket head movement.

I have always liked Gonzales's hammer-the-nail advice because it reinforces what I have been saying all along about stroking technique: you don't have to work that hard to hit a strong shot, even on the serve. *Particularly* on the serve. My guess is that three-fourths of you reading this right now could improve your serve by more than fifty percent, if you were to do just two things:

1. Simplify your service motion.
2. Make better use of the racket head in the swing.

Accomplishing these two objectives will give your serve more consistency, more control and more pace. Best of all, you won't be wearing yourself out so much on the stroke. Here's where Gonzales had the big edge over a lot of big servers today. Some players work so hard on their services that they start to lose some of the power after the first set.

Gonzales was different. He was just as likely to ace you in the fifth set as he was in the first set. His serving motion was so effortless, it didn't tire him out.

There's another reason for developing a more effortless serving motion. It will save wear and tear on your arm. Most of the arm and shoulder problems that intermediate tennis players suffer from can be traced to an unnatural serving motion.

Dennis in Service Standing Position.

Developing a Better Serving Technique

Good serving begins with assuming the right grip and the right starting position. Normally I don't make too big an issue about grips, but on the serve at least, I like to see players use the Continental grip. Spin is the key to controlling a serve, and a Continental grip allows you to impart spin easier than an Eastern forehand grip does.

In singles, it's usually best to line up as close to the center line as you can. This places you as close to the service box on the other side of the court as possible. In doubles, it's better to move a yard or so toward the sideline. This cuts down the amount of open court your opponent can return to. It also offers you a more direct route to the proper volleying position.

Wherever you set up, make certain that your weight is evenly balanced. Do what feels the best for you. In any case, always face somewhat, and perhaps even almost squarely, toward the sideline on the same side as your serving arm.

The main technical problem on the serve is to coordinate the toss with the swing. Two mistakes occur most frequently among club players. One, a lot of players rush the toss and the swing. Two, a lot of players serve as if the toss and the swing were two entirely separate movements. They're not. The two should be done together.

The simplest way I've found to coordinate the toss and the swing is to pretend you're leading a cheer. You simply make the motion that people make when they shout "Hooray." Except for one thing. You do it in slow motion.

The "hooray" motion brings the racket back into a position from which you can generate virtually all the power and control you need. Your knuckles should be facing the back fence. Your wrist should be slightly cocked. Many teaching pros recommend that you drop the wrist at this stage of the swing so that the racket head falls into what everybody calls the "back scratch" position. I'm not saying it's *wrong* to let the racket fall back there. I just don't think it's necessary to think much about it. If your wrist is nice and relaxed when you're taking the racket back to the "hooray" position, the racket head will drop down on its own. You won't have to think about it.

Executing the hooray position takes care of all the little technicalities that make for a successful serving motion. You don't have to worry about where the elbow goes, or how close the arm brushes the body, or how much you rotate the shoulder. Just "hooray" slowly, smoothly and relaxed.

Adding the Toss

So much for the easy part. Now let's talk about the toughest part of serving: tossing the ball. It's one thing to hammer a nail. It's another

Photo of Dennis in "Hooray" Position. **45**

thing to have the nail up there in the same place every time, and that's what good servers do. In order for you to serve consistently, the toss must go to the same place every time.

In the higher levels of tennis, the toss should be pretty much the same, regardless of what sort of a serve you're trying to hit. That's what makes returning against the really good servers so difficult: you can never tell by the toss *where* the ball will come and what sort of a spin it will

Dennis Tossing.

have. Until you can control different types of serves, though, vary the toss according to the type of serve you're trying to hit. For the basic slice serve—this is the serve the pros use most of the time—the toss should reach its projected racket contact zone at a point about a foot or so in front of the baseline, maybe a half a foot or so to the right of your body (left for lefties), and at a height equal to the highest point your racket can reach when you extend your arm straight in the air.

46

47

48

49

How you get the ball up there is your business. If you can get the ball to the same place every time, I don't care how you do it. Still, there are some basic requirements for the toss. It should come up nice and slow, for one, and it should rise with little or no spin. The longer you hold on to the ball as you bring your hand up, the more successful you'll be at accomplishing these two objectives; so try to keep the ball in your hand as long as possible when raising it to the "hooray" position, and don't just chuck it up from your waist or chest heights.

Making Contact

The actual swing on the serve is nothing more than a throwing motion—a *relaxed* throwing motion—with the wrist doing most of the work once the arm motion is halfway completed. Racket head movement—that's what we're aiming for. It is the snapping of the wrist, keyed by your fingers, at the top of the swing, that will actuate the hammer-the-nail motion that will, in turn, generate both power and control.

To hit a flat serve, the racket moves in the same direction as the desired flight of the ball. For a spin serve, the racket should be moving roughly in the direction of the net post, which means that in order to direct the ball into the right court the racket head must glance across the back surface of the ball. This method of making contact will generate spin and will enable you to clear the net by a margin higher than is possible in the flat serve. It is important, though, that you make contact with the ball *before* it has dropped down too far.

Stay relaxed. Many players stay loose throughout the early part of the service motion, but tighten up at the last minute. Don't make the same mistake. Also, be sure to keep your head *up* until the ball has been hit. Dropping the head too soon is another common serving fault. Finally, if you can remember to keep the tossing hand extended in the air a second or two instead of letting it drop down, you'll find it a good aid to holding your balance.

A Learning Sequence for a Better Serve

If you were to come to me for a lesson in serving, here is pretty much the routine I would follow. If you can get a racket and go over it with me, it might be easier for you.

THE HALF-SWING POSITION. Start with the racket in the "hooray" position, and with your gripping hand down at the butt end. Loosen up on the grip so that there is just enough firmness to keep the racket from falling out of your hand. Your wrist should be nice and flexible.

This is how I want you to try to serve some balls the next time you're practicing on a court. Maintaining this abbreviated position, toss the ball the way you normally do, and don't do anything more than simply guide the strings to the ball. Nothing else. Just let the racket head come around easily, as if it were a hammer and you were tapping a picture nail into a fragile wall. Don't worry about power. Don't worry about where the ball is going—whether the serve is good or not. Just get a feel of the racket head alone doing the job.

If you're like most intermediate players I've worked with, you have a surprise in store. The surprise will come when you realize how fast the ball comes off the racket, even though you're hardly gripping the racket, even though you're hardly swinging.

Practice a lot of serves this way. Forget power and direction. Let the racket be a hammer, and the ball a nail.

GETTING A BETTER GRIP. After hitting serves from the abbreviated position, assume your serving grip, but don't tighten up the arm or the wrist. Use the same easy motion you've been using up to now. Grip the racket only as firmly as you have to in order to keep it from flying out of your hands. Serve this way for about five or ten minutes.

Adding the Full Swing. Once you can start controlling the serve by using the techniques described in Step 2, you're ready to incorporate the full swing. Start off in the proper starting position: feet and shoulders toward the sideline, the body well balanced. Now go through the "hooray" motion, in slow motion, and without tossing the ball. Do it several times: just the motion, not the actual tossing of the ball. After you've done this, add the toss, but don't actually swing at the ball. Try to toss the ball to more or less the same place every time, about the height of the racket when it's held outstretched above your head.

Now start to hit the ball. *Not hard.* Free and smooth, the wrist generating the racket head movement. Stay balanced and relaxed.

I cannot emphasize enough the importance of smoothness and rhythm on the serve. This, not how hard you swing, is what produces the power. Focus on balance, fluidity, and letting the racket head hammer the nail, and the power will come.

IMPROVING YOUR SERVING TECHNIQUE IN SIX WEEKS

The serve may be one of the most difficult strokes to master in tennis, but it's the easiest to practice. If it's a problem in your game, you have only yourself to blame. Develop a sound technique. Anybody can get the ball into the box after a while, but the challenge is to control the serve with a technique that will allow you continually to build improvement into the stroke.

Watching Better Players

If you were going to model your serve after any one player, I would recommend, as you've probably guessed by now, Pancho Gonzales. The trouble is that Gonzales doesn't compete too much anymore, so that the opportunities for watching him are limited. If you do get a chance to see Gonzales, pay attention to how deliberate, smooth and natural his serving motion is.

Another top player to watch closely on the serve is Ken Rosewall. I know, Rosewall's serve is supposedly the weakest part of his game, but his technique is one that most intermediate players can imitate more easily than other players. Rosewall has a very simple motion, and even though he doesn't serve the ball as hard as some players, he has excellent control with it. And it's a much tougher serve to return than you might think from seeing it from the gallery or on a television screen.

The same thing holds true for Chris Evert. Women, generally, do not have natural serving motions because so few of them have ever really learned how to throw. Chris Evert's serve is compact and simple. Her toss is consistent, she maintains good balance and she gets maximum use out of her racket.

As far as the big servers in the game are concerned, you have to be realistic. As good a server as Roscoe Tanner is, I wouldn't advise any intermediate to follow his model: it would take years and years to master the timing that enables Tanner to hit the ball on the way up. Newcombe and Ashe have big serves, but they hit the ball too hard to represent realistic models for intermediates, even though Ashe is good to watch in that he maintains excellent balance on the serve.

50   51   52

Serving Sequence.

53   54   55

SHADOW STROKING. Whenever you can manage the time (not to mention a high enough ceiling!) go through the basic serving motion—the "hooray" motion—with the idea of developing a feel for a smooth, flowing motion. Spend a few minutes every day working on it.

THE TOSS. Learn to toss the ball to the same place every time and your serve can't help but improve, regardless of anything else you do. A good way to develop a more consistent serve toss is to rig up some sort of target area in your garage or on an outside wall. An inverted empty coffee can, set up at the proper height, is perfect. Each time you practice, go through the preliminaries of service motion—minus the actual swing—with the racket, and try to see how many times in a row you can toss the ball into the target. Another way of practicing the toss is to draw a small target area, a couple of feet or so in diameter, on the ground. Try to toss the ball up so that it falls into the circle.

SEQUENCE PRACTICE. Go through the sequence previously described. You don't actually have to be on a court. In fact, it's better at first if you practice your technique against a fence or a wall. That way you won't be concerned with whether the ball is going in or not. *Strive to make the serving motion smooth and relaxed.* If you can get an open court, practice the same sequence but, again, don't concern yourself so much with getting the ball in, as with a sound serving technique.

Working on your serve can mean a rough period when you're playing actual matches. Nothing is more discouraging in tennis than to lose because of double faults. There are some ways to minimize the problem. One is to focus on new technique with your first serve, and to use your old technique—assuming it's reliable—for your second serve. Ultimately, though, your goal should be to develop a second serve that you can hit almost as hard as your first serve, changing only the amount of spin you try to generate. Curiously enough, it's the easing up on the second serve that causes many players to double fault. It's difficult to be consistent when you change the basic rhythm and timing of your stroke.

A BETTER RETURN OF SERVE

The main reason most intermediate players don't return serves as well as they might is that very few players practice the stroke enough. The return of serve is best thought of as an abbreviated ground stroke. You observe all the same fundamentals—preparation, balance, racket head movement, etcetera—but you make everything a little more compact. The faster the court surface, the more compact the service return stroke has to be. A realistic goal for the intermediate player is to reach a point at which you're not particularly vulnerable to any one type of serve. You should be able to return as consistently off the backhand as you do off the forehand, and you should be able to handle heavily spinning serves as well. The only way you can reach this degree of return of service proficiency, though, is to become familiar enough with different types of serves so that you're not confused by them. It takes time. It takes practice.

Return of Service Technique

The more economical and compact your return of service motion the better. On a very hard

56

57

Forehand Return of Serve.

58

59

60

61

Backhand Return of Serve.

62

63

64

65

66

67

serve, forget about footwork: just get the racket in front and block the ball back with a very firm grip. If you have more time, get your body turned as you would on a normal ground stroke, but cut down a little on your backswing. Let your wrist and hand take the racket back but don't take it back quite so far as you would for a regular backhand or forehand. The harder the ball is hit to you, the less you have to do to generate pace on the return. If anything, the return of service stroke is closer to a volley swing than it is to a ground stroke swing.

WATCHING THE BALL. Your eyes should start tracking the serve as soon as the other player starts his service motion. Watch the ball go up, watch it come down, follow it all the way to your racket, if you can. Some intermediate players have trouble with heavily spinning serves, but this is due mainly to a lack of experience. With enough practice and experience, you can eventually reach a point where you can tell how the ball is going to react when it bounces by the way the server swings. The trick to returning a serve with lots of spin is to move *in* on the ball and take it on the rise. You never back up on a heavily spinning serve, because the spin makes the ball speed up after the bounce. Meeting it early neutralizes the impact of the spin.

STAYING RELAXED. Even though you have to intensify your concentration when returning serve, don't stiffen up so much that you can't react quickly. Stay loose throughout your arms and shoulders. Assume a good, well-balanced waiting position, weight slightly forward so that you can move in either direction.

Six Weeks to a Better Service Return

Note: Since there is quite a bit of strategy involved in hitting effective service returns, the improvement program for this stroke will come later in the book, in Chapter V.

A BETTER LOB

Most club players do not lob as well as they should. There are two reasons: (1) most players, especially intermediate players, don't respect the shot enough; (2) hardly anybody practices it enough.

It was Pancho Segura who helped me appreciate the value of the lob. As a younger player, I always played an attacking style of tennis. I always considered the lob a strictly defensive shot. Pancho thought otherwise. He used the lob as a means of tiring his opponent. He used it as a way of disrupting the rhythm of the other player.

In high-level tennis, the key to effective lobbing is disguise: keeping your opponent guessing until the last second as to whether you're going to lob or not. Disguise is only possible, of course, when you have the time to choose between a lob and a passing shot. If you can disguise the lob effectively, you can turn it into an offensive weapon. Then it becomes much more than a safety-valve shot: the shot you hit when you're out of position and need time to recover, or when there's no other way to get the ball back.

Lobbing Techniques

The lob, in general, calls for the same fundamentals as a forehand or backhand drive. Early racket preparation, balance, racket head movement—they all play an important role in the lob. Meeting the ball in front is also very important on the lob. The only thing that really differentiates it from the drive is the relationship of the racket to the ball on contact. You hit under the ball and lift up.

Forehand Lob.

68

69

70

71

72

56

73

Backhand Lob.

74

75

77

76

78

79

Most players just don't hit their lobs high enough. Except in some indoor facilities with nonlob ceilings, it hardly matters how *high* the ball goes. As long as it stays on the court, it's a good shot. So don't be afraid to hit it up. Usually when a lob goes out, it's not because you've hit it too hard, but because you didn't get under the ball enough.

Improving Your Lob in Six Weeks

The lob is not a difficult shot to incorporate into your game. You simply make up your mind that you're going to use the shot much more than you've been using it up to now. When you're working on the stroke, practice from both sides and concentrate on two things: getting it high enough, and getting it deep enough. Being able to hit lobs consistently, so that they land within a couple of feet of the baseline, is an extremely valuable weapon in tennis. It's worth working for.

Watching Better Players

If you want to see good lobbing, watch good doubles. Notice how smoothly a good lobber hits the stroke and how well he disguises it. There are several players around today with good top-spin lobs, especially Manuel Orantes, but the top-spin lob is a difficult stroke to master, and I wouldn't start worrying about it until I had a sound defensive lob. Pay close attention to the *height* that good players get on their lobs. Keep it in mind when you're thinking of using more lobs during a match.

Solo Drills

ON COURT.   Set aside ten or fifteen minutes a week to practice lobs on your own. Take a basket of balls and hit lobs from different areas of the backcourt, bouncing the ball first and hitting from both forehand and backhand. Establish target areas right from the beginning. Set goals. Try initially to hit ten lobs in a row in between the service line and the baseline. Then reduce the target areas gradually. Your ultimate goal should be to hit at least ten lobs in a row out of your hand that land in court no farther from the baseline than three or four feet. Hit the ball high, and practice both crosscourt and down the line.

Rallying Drills

LOB/OVERHEAD.   The best way to practice lobbing is to let one player work on the lob while the other player works on overheads. To get the most out of this drill, keep a basket of balls in the back of the court. If you're playing in the backcourt, start out with two or three balls in your hand. Concentrate on hitting the ball high. Try as well to keep the ball deep. If the player at the net is hitting overheads from anywhere around or in front of the service line, you're lobbing too shallow.

PRACTICE GAMES.   Play games or a set in which passing shots are not allowed, and the only way to counteract an advance to the net is to lob.

Match Play Application

Forget the notion that the lob is only a desperation shot. Over the next six weeks, make up your mind to hit at least three lobs in every game you play. Work on the shot in the warm-up. Most players don't hit nearly enough lobs when they're warming up. The lob is a "feel" shot. If you don't develop the feel before you start, it's tough to develop it during the match. Hit backhand lobs as well as forehand lobs. In matches, hit the lob even if your opponent hasn't come to net. Hitting the lob when there is no pressure will help you develop a feel for the shot, and this will come in handy when you're under attack and time comes to hit the shot.

THE OVERHEAD

Most intermediates have difficulty with the overhead, and I'm not surprised. It's the hardest shot in tennis to time, and an inconvenient shot to practice. Like the lob, the overhead is one stroke that very few players practice enough.

All the fundamentals we've been stressing up to now take on special importance when we talk about the overhead. The biggest single cause of overhead errors in the intermediate game is poor preparation. Too many players try to hit the ball as they're backpedaling. As a result, they're off-balance and they're meeting the ball when it's behind them. To hit the overhead well, you must be in a balanced position that will enable you to hit the ball *in front* of you. It is virtually impossible, unless you're a contortionist, to hit a good overhead once the ball has gotten behind you. So part of the stroking technique involves getting an early jump on the ball. This, in turn, involves being *alert* to the possibility of the lob. Too many players approach the net as if the lob were an illegal stroke, racing so quickly toward the net that in the event the ball *is* lobbed, they can't recover quickly enough to get back in time. When you're moving up to the net, you naturally want to move as quickly as you can, but not so helter-skelter that you can't react to the lob.

Hitting the Overhead Better

If you have a consistent problem with the overhead, the chances are you're not getting the racket back soon enough. If you watch good players hit the overhead, the first thing you'll see them do is to get the racket back. The racket

is already back, as they're moving back under the ball. They don't wait until they've positioned themselves before bringing the racket back.

What do I mean by "back"? The ready position I recommend on the overhead is almost the same as the "hooray" position we've already talked about on the serve.

This is the position you want to be in as the ball is coming down. To be in position already as the ball is descending, you must get a quick start. A second or two can make a big difference. It takes time to be able to judge where you should position yourself under a lob—especially a very high one—but this ability comes with practice. The best place to make contact on the overhead is as high as you can comfortably extend the racket and in front—about the place you'd want to hit the ball if you were serving. You have to be aggressive with the shot. If you wait until the ball has dropped too far, you'll hit it into the net.

The motion I recommend for hitting the overhead is the same "hammer-the-nail" motion we talked about on the serve. Not too much arm, but a healthy amount of racket head movement. Don't try to kill the ball. You'll miss more than you make. Let the wrist do the heavy work. Keep your head up. Jerking the head down too soon is a big reason so many overheads land in the net.

Something else, too. There's no law in tennis that says you can't let the lob bounce first before you hit it. Actually, it's not a good policy to hit a very high—and deep—defensive lob on the fly, especially on a very sunny or windy day. On lobs that are not unusually high and look as if they're going to land fairly shallow—anywhere

The Overhead.　　　　　　　80　　　　　　　　　　　81　　　　　　　　　　　82

from the service line to the net—try to hit the ball on a fly. Anything higher or deeper, play it more conservatively. It's just as easy to put away the lob after a bounce as it is on the fly.

Six Weeks to a Better Overhead Technique

The only way to develop a good overhead is to spend as much time as you can spare just practicing the shot. Only by hitting hundreds can you hope to develop the instinct to position yourself properly and acquire the timing that will give you the confidence you need to make the shot consistently. If you can spend a half hour a week for six weeks, just practicing nothing but overheads, it will make a difference.

Watching Better Players

The pro game is filled with players with good overheads. The main thing to look for when you're watching the pros hit is how quickly they start to move back on the lob and how automatically the racket gets back. Watch, too, the way certain players track the ball. Arthur Ashe, for instance, likes to use his free hand, the index finger extended, to line up the ball as it drops. Another thing to observe is the aggressiveness with which the better players hit the shot. It isn't so much hitting the ball hard, but hitting it early enough and with enough racket head movement. Rosewall proves the point very well. He has one of the best overheads in tennis, but never makes the mistake of overmuscling the ball.

Solo Drills

SHADOW STROKING. Here's a good conditioning and technique drill you can do on your own, as long as you're not self-conscious about other

83   **84**   **85**

people watching you. Imagine that you're in a rally against an opponent who is trying to lob you to death. You move to the net, react to the lob, move back quickly, and go through the stroking motion. Concentrate, in particular, on getting the racket back early. I frequently follow this drill when I'm working with a group of players on one court. I like it because it gets you accustomed to moving with the racket already back—one of the keys to a successful overhead.

Rallying Drills

SEQUENCE PRACTICE. Working with a ball machine or a friend, try to develop some overhead consistency by practicing the stroke in sequence. Begin first with lobs hit right at you and with the racket already back. Then move the lobs a little deeper, which means you'll have to move back, the racket still back. Once you can hit the stroke with the racket already back, start from the normal ready position but follow the same procedure: easy lobs at first, more difficult lobs later. Concentrate on meeting the

ball early and high with the hammer-the-nail stroke. Don't worry about *where* you hit it. Focus on meeting it cleanly. Don't overhit.

Match Play Application

Developing your overhead through match play competition is hard because the only way you can hit the shot is if your opponent lobs. One possible answer to this dilemma is to play somebody from whom you can expect a lot of lobbing. Another way is to come to the net a lot more than you normally do. In any event, make sure you get a lot of overhead practice during the warm-up. If you usually spend ten minutes warming up for your weekly doubles game, spend half of that time practicing overheads.

ADDING STROKES TO YOUR REPERTOIRE: THE HALF VOLLEY AND THE DROP SHOT

Some strokes in tennis cannot be thought of as "fundamental," but are still important to develop, once you've mastered the basic strokes. The two I'm concerned with here are the half volley and the drop shot.

HITTING A BETTER HALF VOLLEY

The half volley is not a shot you go out of your way to hit. It's basically a defensive shot— a reaction to a ball that's bouncing right at your feet. Yet, if you want to play serve and volley tennis against good players, this is a shot you are pretty much forced to develop. A player who can return serve will frequently try to place his returns right at your feet. If the shot is hit well enough, the only thing you can do with the ball is half volley it.

Half-Volleying Technique

The half volley is a more difficult shot than you might think from watching some of the pros hit it. The top players—people like Ilie Nastase and Brian Gottfried—make the shot look very easy, as if all they're doing is getting the racket into the path of the ball, but the appearance is deceptive. The reason good players make the shot look easy is that they get into position early, maintain good balance and avoid the mistake that most intermediate players make with the half volley, which is to overhit.

The key point to focus on when you're working on your half volley is body position. You have to do more with the shot than simply drop the racket head. Your whole body has to get down, the knees well bent, the racket head level. But even though you're crouched down, you still have to stay relaxed. Only then can you execute the smooth, short stroke that's needed to control the ball on the half volley.

Two other points are important to remember on the half volley. One is to watch the ball very carefully. A lot of players make the mistake of lifting their heads too soon. You must watch the ball all the way to the racket, keeping your head down until contact is made. Secondly, you mustn't overhit. The half volley is more than a block, but it's not as full a stroke as a ground stroke. Here, again, the racket head has to do the work, not the arm and not the body. You meet the ball as far in front as you can comfortably manage, with the racket head slightly open. The follow-through is fairly short, but it's smooth.

Six Weeks to a Better Half Volley

Developing a better half volley in the case of most intermediate players usually involves two things: one is the ability to get down into the proper hitting position quickly and with good balance; the other is the proper racket work. The drills suggested here are keyed to both of these fundamentals.

Solo Drills

SHADOW STROKING. Shadow-stroking drills are especially valuable when you're working to improve your half volley, because much of your ability to hit the stroke successfully is tied into balance and body control. Try to set aside a few minutes a day, at home or at the court, going

86

87

Dennis Demonstrating Half Volley.

88

89

90

91

through the motions of the stroke, backhand and forehand, concentrating on your balance as you bend your body low. You should find that within two or three weeks it will take less effort than before to get into position. This improvement alone should help to give you more control with the stroke.

BOUNCE AND HIT. Practice hitting half volleys out of your hand by bouncing the ball and making contact a few inches off the ground. Make sure you bend your knees and stay relaxed throughout the stroke. Work on both forehand and backhand, and hit the stroke from various positions on the court.

Rallying Drills

The problem with practicing the half volley in rallying drills is that you need a partner who can consistently place the ball at your feet. That's quite a lot to ask. A good way to deal with this problem is to stop rallying for a while and have your partner either throw or hit balls hard to you that land right at your feet. Positioning yourself at the service line should help. When you're practicing the shot, work initially on control—getting it back. Once you can return the shot with a reasonable amount of consistency, try to control the direction of it and later work on depth. A workable goal on the half volley is to hit ten consecutive shots that land beyond your opponent's service line.

Match Play Application

Since the half volley is not a shot you go out of your way to hit, it's a difficult shot to practice

Forehand and Backhand Drop Shots.

during an actual match. You might try letting some low volleys bounce first before hitting them as a way of getting more practice under pressure, but your best strategy is to work on the stroke in practice, as a sort of insurance policy, but do your best to avoid the shot in match play.

THE DROP SHOT

Players, like myself, who grew up using hard courts, have never concentrated much on the drop shot, but now that more and more tournaments are being played on slower surfaces, the stroke is becoming more important. My feeling about the drop shot is that it's a good shot to have, but not a stroke you should overuse. The drop shot works best when it takes your opponent by surprise. To use it over and over robs the shot of the surprise element.

Drop Shot Technique

The drop shot is best thought of as an exaggerated slice shot. It's a touch shot, but it's still a full stroke. There is a tendency among some players to *under*hit the drop shot—to hit the ball too weakly. You achieve shallowness on the drop shot less by power in the swing than by the angle of the racket face on contact. The ball is met with a sharp down thrust and with the racket more open than it would be for a slice shot.

Six Weeks to a Better Drop Shot

The drop shot is not an easy stroke to master by any means, and even after you've mastered it, you have to practice it continuously if you want to use it effectively. A combination of drilling and match play application can produce the necessary feel and confidence, but you're not going to develop the shot overnight.

Watching Better Players

The players with the best drop shots in tennis are generally the players who've grown up on clay—in particular, Europeans like Ilie Nastase and Manuel Orantes. Among the women, Chris Evert has perhaps the best drop shot, mainly because she uses it so effectively. The deeper you keep your ground strokes normally, the more effective you can be with your drop shot, and Chris Evert, who gets excellent depth with her ground strokes, is the perfect illustration. Players like Orantes and Nastase use the drop shot in many cases to draw baseline top-spinners, like Borg and Vilas, closer to the net, where they can't hurt you so much. Their idea is not to win the point outright on the shot, but to set their opponent up for a passing shot.

Solo Drills

BOUNCE AND HIT. Station yourself at the service line with a basket of balls. Practice forehand and backhand drop shots, concentrating initially on hitting each shot so that it doesn't land beyond the service line on the other side of the net. Gradually bring your target areas in closer until you can hit ten good drop shots in a row that land no more than three feet from the net and bounce at least three times before reaching the service line.

Rallying Drills

CONTROL. You and your partner should station yourselves at each service line opposite each other. See how many successful drop shots you can hit to each other. Set an initial goal of five each. Work up to twelve.

CONSISTENCY. Rally from the baseline with the idea that either you or your partner hit a drop shot on any ball that bounces on the service line or closer to the net. Strive in the beginning to clear the net on every stroke. Once you can clear the net, concentrate on hitting it shallow.

GAME DRILLS. Play a set in which each player must hit a drop shot on every ball that bounces on the service line or closer to the net. (Don't deliberately hit balls shallow, except for the drop shot.)

Match Play Application

A good way to improve your drop shot is to play against weaker players, who hit a lot of shallow shots. Whereas you might normally want to attack on those short balls, practice the drop shot instead, following the sequence we talked about under Bounce and Hit solo drills: first, getting the ball over the net and then getting the ball to land closer and closer to the net.

A LOOK AT SPIN

Up to now I haven't talked much about spin, but it's something we're obviously going to have to get into—particularly since there is so much talk today about top spin. I find myself occasionally working with beginners who are interested *only* in hitting the ball with more top spin, as if top spin were the ultimate answer to tennis success.

I would never suggest that spin does not have its place in tennis, but spin can only work for you once you've mastered the other fundamentals in your strokes. You generate spin—underspin or top spin—by changing the angle of the racket head on contact. You impart slice or underspin by coming down and across the ball. You impart top spin by hitting up and over the ball. In any case, you still have to get ready early, you still need a well-balanced position, you still have to watch the ball, and you still have to generate racket head movement.

An important aspect of spin is knowing when to use it. Despite the fact that players with heavily top-spin shots—a Borg, for example, or a Vilas—do well, I don't recommend a heavily top-spin shot for a basic forehand or backhand drive. First, it's a more difficult shot to hit, and so it takes a longer time to develop steady top-spin shots than to develop steady shots that are hit either flat or with a small amount of top spin. Second, coming over the ball time after time puts a lot of wear and tear on your wrist and arm. And, finally, unless you can really pound the ball the way Borg, Vilas, or Laver do, the top-spin drive from the baseline is not going to give you enough depth to make the shot effective.

Top spin, if you can manage it, works well for passing shots. Depth isn't too important on passing shots; also the dipping action of the ball makes it a little harder to volley than a flat shot. Top spin is useful in those situations where the ball is bouncing fairly close to the net and your opponent is in the forecourt. Here the problem is getting enough pace on the ball to pass your opponent and still keep the ball on the court. A little rolled top-spin shot does the job very nicely.

Underspin has different uses. I've already pointed out the value of some underspin on volleys, but I also like to see players hitting their approach shots with some underspin. Underspin takes pace off the ball but gives you a little more control. A ball hit with underspin will tend to bounce low and skid a little, making it a tougher shot off which to hit a strong passing shot. Underspin can also work to your advantage if you're blocking back a very hard-hit serve.

You do not have to change your basic technique drastically in order to generate either top spin or underspin on your shots. To put a little more top spin into your shots, follow all the basic steps you normally would, but start your swing from a slightly lower position and let the racket head come up and over the ball more.

As far as underspin shots go, start the swing a little higher, tilt the racket slightly upward on contact, and follow through as you normally do.

The only way to master these spin variations is—you guessed it!—practice and more practice.

SOME FINAL THOUGHTS ON TECHNIQUE

We've just gone through the main strokes in tennis, focusing on those features that I consider to be the most fundamental. The fundamentals I stress apply almost equally to all the strokes. Early preparation, balance, and racket head movement all play as big a role in ground strokes as they do on volleys and overheads. I realize I haven't talked much about some of the other things that many teaching professionals and other instructional manuals deal with, like grips and footwork. I agree that footwork is extremely important and, for some players, that grips can make a major difference. What I've tried to do, though, is to key in on those areas that you can most easily incorporate into your own style in a six-week program geared to raise your level of tennis. Regardless of how you're hitting the ball now, you can do it better if you can get ready a little sooner, hit with a little more balance, and let the racket head do more work. A little later in the book, we'll talk about how to use these improvements in your technique to better advantage. In the next chapter, however, we're going to focus on two factors I consider almost as important as technique: quickness and physical conditioning.

A solid technique can only carry you so far in tennis. To get the most out of this technique, you have to be quick on your feet and you have to be in good physical shape. If you have only average strokes, but are quick and in good physical condition, you will generally beat a player with better strokes who isn't quick and isn't in good physical shape. What's more, quickness and physical conditioning present the same opportunities for improvement as your basic shots. That's what this chapter is all about.

YOU'RE QUICKER THAN YOU THINK

Most tennis players think of quickness in terms of two things: speed and reflexes. I see it in a larger context: the ability to be ready early.

I can guess what you're thinking: that getting ready early is, in fact, a matter of speed and reflexes: the reflexes to get you to react quickly, the speed to get you to the ball.

The trouble with talking about "getting ready" purely in terms of speed and reflexes is that it promotes the idea that quickness is either something you have or you don't have, something you're born with, like the color of your eyes. It's not. You can improve quickness, just as you can improve your serve or your volley. It's a matter of knowing what's involved, and knowing how to go about it.

THE ELEMENTS OF QUICKNESS

Quickness, by my definition, takes in two elements: anticipation and movement. Anticipation means the same thing on the court that it means off the court: thinking ahead, getting ready for the next shot as soon as you've completed the stroke. Movement means the special kind of movement that works for tennis: smooth, balanced movement.

4

Getting Quicker and Shaping Up

69

THE ESSENCE OF ANTICIPATION

You may be able to run the length of a tennis court twice as fast as I can, but if I start only three feet from the ball, and you're six feet from it, we're going to both get to the ball at the same time. Here, in a nutshell, is what anticipation is all about: knowing enough about the dynamics of position to minimize the amount of court you have to cover to get to each ball early.

Let me differentiate here between anticipation at the basic level and anticipation at the advanced levels of the game. Experienced players usually have a fair idea of where their opponents are going to hit the ball. You never *really* know, of course, but if you've played somebody many times, you have a fair idea of where he likes, say, to hit his passing shots, or what he likes to do with his smashes—things like that. Occasionally, you can get crossed up: a player will hit a shot you simply are not expecting. But if you're a percentage player—and most professionals are—you don't worry too much about the unexpected shots. You anticipate the percentage shot.

But let's not worry too much here about the advanced levels of anticipation. Most intermediate players haven't yet adopted *basic* anticipation techniques into their games. Most don't appreciate the real meaning and the importance of good court position.

To explain what I mean by position, let me introduce a simple concept. We'll call it "home base." "Home base" is the place you generally want to be at the moment your opponent makes contact with the ball. It's the place on the court from which you have the best chance of getting

to the majority of the shots your opponent hits.

Usually, you'll only have to concern yourself with two such places. The basic "home base" position is dead center close to the baseline. From this position, you can reach most shots. In the forecourt, the "home base" I like to use is three to four feet inside the service line straddling the line that separates the service boxes. Positioning yourself here gives you a reasonable chance at passing shots hit to either side and allows you to cover all but the most expertly hit lobs.

You have some flexibility here. If you're up against an opponent who hits the ball consistently deep, move back a couple of steps. Against a player who never lobs, move in a few steps. If he's a player who always goes the same way on his passing shots, edge over to that side.

The main thing, however, is to get in this position early enough. The only way to do this is to start moving into position right after you've hit your shot. So many players make the mistake of standing there after they've hit the ball—standing and looking to see where their ball is going.

Good players don't. Good players start to move back into position *as soon as they've finished the shot.* You can't always do it, but most of the time you have enough time between the moment you've finished your stroke and the moment your opponent makes his return to move into the "home base" position. You do, that is, if you train yourself to move right away, to "think quick."

One of the best ways to reinforce the importance of getting back into position after each shot is to watch the professionals in action, especially the great baseliners like Ken Rosewall, Björn Borg, and Chris Evert. Watch what they do *after* they hit the ball—how they're always shuffling back to a more or less central position along the baseline.

Moving back into position after every shot doesn't come naturally. You have to practice it, make it into a habit. Hit and move. Hit and move. There's no reason to be caught frequently out of position—in that "no-man's-land," for instance, between the baseline and the service line—more than a couple of times a set. Forget the ball you've just hit. Train yourself to start moving into position for each new shot. Everything I've said about anticipation in singles applies equally to doubles. The only problem is, it's not so easy to establish a "home base" concept in doubles as it is in singles. You'll rarely see a good doubles player standing still in the course of point. Regardless of whether he's involved in the exchange or not, a good doubles player is always moving, always anticipating—cutting down the best angles of returns from the other side. This may not be the place to delve too deeply into the fine points of doubles positioning, but I'd like to emphasize a couple of basic points here anyway.

Advanced doubles is primarily a battle for the net. The team that commands the net in doubles usually wins the point. Some net positions, however, are better than others—better in the sense that they more effectively limit the options of your opponents. It is one thing if you and your partner occupy more or less central positions on each side of the court—let's say, in the middle of each service box—and the ball is deep in your opponent's court but down the center. But this position is not the most advantageous if the ball is deep in one of your opponents' corners. In this situation, good percentage tennis dictates that the two of you both move *toward* the sideline that bounds that corner. Doing so is a matter of geometry and angles. It cuts down both the amount of down-the-line court space available for a passing shot against you, and also the size of the open space in your court that's relatively easy to hit. The dynamics in doubles are more complicated than in singles, but we're still talking here about "hitting and moving." Understanding these dynamics can turn you into a better tennis player virtually overnight. It explains why experienced, older

doubles players can frequently beat teams who are younger, quicker and who hit harder, and why sometimes it's even true when an older player upsets a younger one in singles.

SIX WEEKS TO BETTER ANTICIPATION

Anticipation involves mental discipline as much as physical skill. Knowing where you should be after every shot is one thing. Remembering to go there is another. A good deal of this is habit—habits that can be developed through drills.

Watching Better Players

All the pro players anticipate well. That's why the shots many pros hit often look so easy to spectators. When you watch a pro match, notice how each player gets back into position after each shot and how doing this gives him or her additional time to move to the next shot without hurry. In doubles, focus on one team—and nearly all the successful doubles teams, John Newcombe–Tony Roche, Stan Smith–Bob Lutz, Bob Hewitt–Frew McMillan, are interesting to watch. Note where they position themselves at different stages of the point. Notice how they move from side to side, and when they retreat to the baseline. Notice, finally, how each player seems to "know" where his partner is, even without looking. Good doubles players rarely have to look over their shoulders to see what their partners are up to. Positioning becomes a team effort, each player knowing where his partner is on the basis of where he himself is and where the ball is.

Solo Drills

ON COURT HOME BASE. This solo drill is excellent for reinforcing the idea of moving back into position after every shot. Set up a basket of balls in the center of the court along the baseline. Take a ball from the basket, move quickly to one side or the other and bounce/hit a forehand or backhand. Then return for another ball, and move to another area along the baseline. Move quickly but simulate match conditions—shuffling back to the basket as if you were awaiting the next shot from the other player. Hit the ball. Don't slap.

Rallying Drills

THE HOME BASE DRILL. Imagine a circle around the midpoint line along the baseline, think of this circle as home base. Rally with your partner, hitting forehands and backhands, but always return to this position after every shot. Get into the habit of not standing and looking to see where *your* ball went. Instead move immediately toward the position that will better prepare you for the return.

Match Play Application

SINGLES. During your warm-up, fixate on a specific area along the baseline and tell yourself right from the start that there is where you're going to be moving after every ground stroke. Do it during the warm-up. Keep telling yourself "Hit and Move." *"Hit and Move."* "HIT AND MOVE!" Even in the warm-up, get out of the habit of watching your shots to see where they go.

DOUBLES. Take a few minutes before your doubles matches to discuss with your partner your movement patterns. Keep the guidelines simple. Generally, the two of you should be moving in tandem, advancing to the net when you've hit deep forcing shots or deep lobs, retreating in tandem when the ball is deep in your own backcourt.

At the same time, though, don't make the mistake of overstepping your capabilities. If you're not a good volleyer, you don't have to station yourself close to the net when your partner is serving and you certainly ought to move farther back on a second serve. Work *with* each other. If you don't have confidence in your overhead, let your partner hit most lobs but make sure you cover the position he's left vacant. It's usually not ideal, but it's okay in doubles if one of you is back and the other is at the net, as long as the two of you are not on the same side of the court. Communication—that's the key to a successful doubles team. You should know pretty much where your partner is going to be serving and you should know, too, when your partner is going to poach. Many doubles teams have signals they give each other before each point. Anything you can do to give your partner a better idea of what you're going to try to do will reduce the chances of the two of you being caught out of position.

MOVING BETTER

Until recently, not many people in tennis gave much thought to the actual mechanics of movement, but lately a lot of players have been taking special movement coaching.

I think this new appreciation for movement is a good thing. The better you move, the easier it's going to be for you to get to the ball early and to set up a well-balanced ready position. My only question is whether it's possible to set down specific techniques for running, and apply them to every player. Movement strikes me as being a very personal thing—each player running in his or her own style.

But this doesn't alter the basic fact that most intermediate players don't move nearly so well as they might if they were to concentrate a little more on improving this particular aspect of their game.

The Essence of Movement

Moving well in tennis is less a matter of sheer speed than it is a matter of smoothness and balance. I can think of any number of players I've known who were a good thirty pounds overweight, and yet covered the court well because they were light on their feet. It isn't usually necessary to run at full speed. Even on drop shots, you have more time to get to the ball than you might think—as long as you start moving *early* enough.

Remember, a tennis court is not a football field. It is only nine yards from one singles sideline to the other, and only thirteen yards from the baseline to the net. From the center of the court along the baseline you need make no more than four or five steps to get to most balls. You don't have to run flat out to get to those balls, either. More than run, you want a kind of *glide* to the ball. Move lightly, and in balanced steps. Never run helter-skelter or in long pounding strides.

Another key element to attainment of court mobility is balance. If you can stay well balanced as you're running, it's going to be that much easier for you to set up a well-balanced hitting position. Good balance as you run is best achieved by keeping your movements simple, by minimizing the degree of arm and head movement as you run.

But I can't tell you how to run, or how to maintain your balance. All I can do is emphasize the importance of balance and agility when you're moving to the ball, and suggest some drills that might help you. Each person, in the end, has to move in a manner that best suits him or her. Quicker players tend to move in short, rapid steps instead of long strides, but if you have the ability to move in long strides and still keep your balance, by all means, keep it up.

The Warm-Up

Let's start with what I consider one of the most neglected areas in tennis: the warm-up. By warm-up, I mean a regular routine of stretching exercises before you even step on the court.

If you think that the sort of warm-up I'm talking about here is only for top level tournament players, you're wrong. If anything, a good warm-up is perhaps more important to the weekend player than to the professional. Unlike a professional, the average weekend player doesn't train everyday. Consequently, the right sort of warm-up can make an enormous difference in a player's chances of avoiding any number of muscle injuries tennis players are prone to suffer. I would even venture to guess that the injuries of club players would be cut down by eighty to ninety percent if everyone took a few minutes before playing in order to warm up properly.

There is another dimension to a proper warm-up that isn't directly related to injuries. If you start to play before you've warmed up properly, chances are your timing will not be tuned up and your movements will be sluggish. And since very few club players take the time to hit enough balls in the warm-up, you're going to get off to a bad start. Some players aren't bothered if their shots aren't going in at first, but with other players a poor start produces anger and frustration. You start getting down on yourself right from the beginning. "Oh, no. I'm having another one of those days," you start saying to yourself. Your confidence disappears. You get angrier and angrier with each passing minute, and before you know it, your hour or hour and a half is up, and you've had a miserable time.

I don't guarantee that the right sort of warm-up will totally eliminate those kinds of days, but I think it will help decrease their frequency. Ten minutes of the right kind of exercises before playing will make your body feel looser and better. It will help to get your mind on the right track as well. If you're like most people, you need a transition between the life you live off the court and the things you hope to do on the court. A regular, systematized warm-up serves the function very well.

Do it. Get into the habit of arriving ten minutes earlier than you normally do for tennis. Spend those ten minutes doing the simple exercises I'm about to recommend. Treat them as part of your overall tennis routine, as much a part of your tennis as tying your shoelaces. The exercises are not difficult. They're not rigorous. But they *can* make a difference.

The sequence for warm-up exercises I've listed here is based in part on a series of warm-up exercises developed by the track coach Henry Hines. It is one I use and that many of the professionals use as well. The routine is designed to limber up all of the major muscle groups used in tennis.

BREAKING A SWEAT. Start out by running easily around the court, or else jogging in place, just long enough to heat your body up. Be relaxed. Don't run fast or get pooped.

WINDMILLING. Start out with your hands straight in front. Bring both arms straight up and around in windmill fashion—and stretching slowly. Try to feel the blood flowing through your fingertips. Do this ten times from front to back, then reverse the sequence. Next, loosen up the arms and pivot your body around back and forth letting the arms swing out very loosely at each side. Again, try to feel the blood flowing into your fingers. Do this for about thirty seconds. Windmilling exercises are especially important if you are prone to arm and shoulder injuries. Remember to stay loose and relaxed throughout.

NECK STRETCH. Stand relaxed with your hands at your side. Tilt only your head slowly to one side and make a circle. Bring it back to the starting position. Repeat this three or four times slowly, then go through the same procedure in the other direction, down, and finally, up. This exercise is meant to loosen up the neck muscles. Stay relaxed as you do it.

HAMSTRING STRETCH. Flexible hamstring muscles are important for mobility. To get them loose, stand with your feet together and bend over slowly, keeping your knees as straight as possible. Try to touch the tips of your shoes with the tips of your fingers. If you can't make it, go down as far as you can, so that you can feel the hamstring muscles being stretched. Hold that position until you count to five and then come up—easy. Repeat the motion a few times, bending a little farther each time, until your fingers touch the ground. *Don't bounce up and down.* This can cause a muscle pull. Do it slowly.

LEG STRETCH. Stand with your feet well apart. Bend over at the waist and without bending your knees, try to touch your right foot with both hands, or come as close as you can, the fingers outstretched. Keep your arms in that position and shift them to the center, and then to the other foot. Repeat this exercise five times,

Dennis Doing Hamstring Stretch.   94

Dennis Demonstrating Leg Stretch.   95

Dennis Demonstrating Hurdler's Stretch.   96

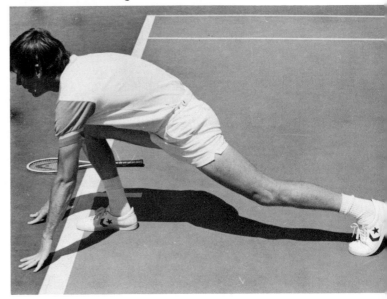

widening the arc you make with each repetition. Be relaxed.

HURDLER'S STRETCH. Stand with your legs comfortably apart, one in front of the other. Bend one knee and lean forward. Keep the other knee as straight as possible. Stretch this way a few times and then cup both hands around your ankle. Repeat several times on the other side.

JUMPING IN PLACE. Stand with your feet close together. Take ten to twenty small jumps on the tips of your toes (as if you were jumping rope), keeping your balance and staying as light on your feet as you can. Then jump a little higher the same number of times. Stop and rest. Finally, jump as high as you can, again the same number of times.

SIX WEEKS TO BETTER MOBILITY

Quickness depends, in large part, on a reasonably high level of coordination and agility, both of which can be improved through a variety of drills and exercises. Since many tennis players

Getting Quicker and Shaping Up

find drills that do not involve a racket and a ball tedious, I have tried to make the following quickness drills as interesting as possible.

Solo Drills

JUMPING ROPE.   One of the best ways I know of to improve general movement skills is to spend at least ten minutes a day jumping rope. Skipping rope lends itself to any number of different routines. One that has worked well for me goes as follows:

You start off jumping with both feet off the ground. Establish an initial goal of ten consecutive jumps without a miss. Then try for ten consecutive jumps on the right foot only, and ten consecutive jumps on the left foot only. Finally, skip alternating your feet.

To get the most of rope skipping, stay as light on your feet as you can. Concentrate on making as little noise as possible when you jump. Once you reach ten jumps without a miss in the various sequences described above, raise your goals gradually. A realistic target within a few weeks of daily jumping should be twenty-five jumps in each sequence—all without a miss. If you miss, you should start over.

The more serious you are about your tennis, the more you should make it a point to jump a little rope everyday. Jumping rope is good for your legs, your wind, your basic agility and your hand/eye coordination. Make sure that the rope you buy is the right size for you. If you stand on the middle of the rope, the ends should extend, evenly on both sides. to about the height of your chest.

JOGGING PLUS.   Jogging by itself is excellent for building up your legs and increasing your stamina, but it won't do much for your quickness unless you can incorporate some specific features. If you're already in the habit of jogging, work in some wind sprints—quick twenty-yard bursts—as well as some side-to-side shuffling and back pedaling. Shuffling, sideways and backward helps to strengthen the upper thigh muscles—muscles that don't get much of a workout when you run normally.

If you can, try to run on a regular running track or on grass. Running on asphalt is tough on the legs and feet.

QUICK FEET DRILL.   Here's a drill that many of the players on the circuit now do regularly, and with good results. The idea is to see how many times you can touch the ground with each foot as you run in place, in a series of ten-second sequences. The easiest way to do this drill is to count each step in sequences of ten: "one-two-three-four-five-six-seven-eight-nine-ONE, one-two-three-four-five-six-seven-eight-nine-TWO, etcetera. A count of five within a ten-second sequence is about average. Anything between seven and nine is very good. Ten or above is super. The best thing about this drill is the way it forces you to get your feet moving faster than you're moving them now, and faster, probably, than you ever imagined you could move them.

SHADOW STROKING.   Working with the racket, set up a two- or three-minute drill in which you simulate a long tennis rally that takes you from one side of the court to the other, to the net and back, etcetera. Simulate each of the strokes in the drill and concentrate on a smooth and well-balanced recovery. Finish up the stroke, regain your balance and move in the other direction.

Rallying Drills

HITTING ON THE RUN.   Build some element of movement into all of your rallying sequences. Instead of remaining in the center of the court after you've hit a ground stroke in a rally, move back to one of the corners. I know this is contrary to my general rule, but in learning to hit on the run it will force you to hustle a few steps to get to the next ball. Do your best to prevent any ball from bouncing more than once. I see intermediate players frequently warming up and not caring very much how many times the ball bounces. I discourage this practice as much as I can with my own students. To get the most out of a practice session, you must simulate match conditions as much as possible.

TWO-ON-ONE DRILLS. Rallying drills to improve movement, work best when you have two players hitting against one. The two players at the net should set up a basket of balls between them and move the player at the baseline back and forth as much as possible. The important thing for the player at the baseline to remember is to hit every ball on the first bounce. Don't get sloppy on this drill. Move early, assume position, hit your stroke and start moving for the next ball. Five minutes or so of this drill is usually enough to exhaust most intermediate players.

ONE-ON-ONE. There are several different one-on-one drills that lend themselves to improving mobility. One I like works like this. One player sets up along the baseline in the center of the court. The other player sets up at the net in the deuce court. The baseliner has to hit the ball every time back to the deuce court. The player at the net can move the ball around from side to side. You then switch roles. Let the baseline player stand in the deuce court and let the other player move from side to side at the net. What's good about this drill is that it forces you to hit your ground strokes to specific spots instead of just hitting randomly. There are several combinations that work. For example, the net man can operate in either the ad or deuce court. Likewise the baseliner. For best results, work on about five minutes for each position.

SINGLES PLUS. Play a set of singles but use the doubles boundaries. If one of the players is noticeably weaker, let him or her use the doubles boundaries while the stronger player uses the singles boundaries. If you're the stronger player,

get into the habit of running down balls that bounce in the alley. If you can run down balls hit in the alley, there's no reason you can't run down most of the balls hit to you in a singles match.

Match Play Application

Earlier in the book, I stressed the idea of quickness being as much in the mind as it is in the body. By now, you should appreciate what I mean. You must "think" quick on the court. This means, for one thing, feeling loose and nimble, staying relaxed and light on your feet. Sometimes in a match, you may *think* you're moving, but you're not. This happens, particularly, in important matches when you're more nervous than you might think. Because your adrenalin is flowing and your heart is beating, you have the feeling that you're moving quickly but actually, you're not moving well at all. One of the best ways to counteract this phenomenon is to be conscious of really picking up your feet as you run. A lot of professional players, as they're awaiting serve, will run in place for a few seconds: this helps to keep your feet moving in concert with your nervous system. It's a good way to minimize the effects of choking.

GETTING INTO BETTER SHAPE

There isn't a good tennis player who doesn't realize the importance of conditioning. I have seen many matches, at all levels of tennis, in which the difference at the end came down to one thing: the winner was in better physical shape.

Getting Quicker and Shaping Up

77

Conditioning affects more than your physical strength throughout a match. It affects your mental toughness, too. Fatigue dims concentration. It changes the rhythm of your game. You get a little tired, and you try to end the points a little earlier. You start to press, to hit harder, and pretty soon the errors mount. You get angry with yourself, and you become more tired still. Your alertness suffers.

The pros set the best example. Ask Arthur Ashe why he had such a great year in 1975 and he'll tell you, without hesitation: "I trained harder. I was in better shape." There isn't a consistent winner on the circuit who doesn't train hard.

SHAPING UP OFF THE COURT

There are any number of articles and books that deal with physical fitness, and since I am not a physical fitness expert, I'm not enough of an authority to prescribe too specific a program. The United States Government publishes an excellent fitness guide called *Adult Physical Fitness*. It costs eighty cents and is available from the U.S. Government Printing Office, Washington, D.C. 20402.

Nearly all the exercises listed in the guide are good for tennis players. Tennis is a sport in which almost every group of muscles has to function well, and this guide offers a program designed to build up all the muscle groups.

Nearly everybody in the fitness field stresses the importance of making exercise a fixed part of your daily routine. I agree. There are an infinite number of ways to structure an exercise

workout, but I think the best approach is to select about ten exercises or so that relate directly to a variety of muscle groups and to do these ten every day.

One of the best workouts I've seen is one I used to use with the U.S. Davis Cup teams. I like it because it combines stamina with muscle conditioning. It's a twelve-minute routine. You do a sequence of twelve exercises, one after another, for one minute each without a rest in between sequences. It works like this:

1. Run for a minute (or run in place for a minute).
2. Do sit-ups for a minute.
3. Run for a minute.
4. Do leg raises for a minute. (You raise your legs together to a 90° position, open and close them, then lower the legs one-third of the way, raise them again, and repeat until the minute is up.)
5. Run for a minute.
6. Do push-ups for a minute.
7. Run for a minute.
8. Do leg stretches for a minute.
9. Run for a minute.
10. Do flutter kicks. (Sit up with legs extended and arms behind you as a brace. Lift both legs off the ground, move them quickly up and down for about ten seconds. Rest for five seconds. Repeat.) This is an excellent stomach conditioner.
11. Run for a minute.
12. Repeat sit-ups for a minute.

Don't be intimidated by this routine. Unless you're in super shape, you won't be able to go through the sequence right away. If you want to try this drill, begin modestly: twenty seconds to each sequence. Then raise it after a few days to thirty seconds, forty, fifty, and so on, until you can handle the full minute per sequence. You can do this drill anywhere, at home, in your office or hotel room. But to get the best results from it, do it every day.

Other Recommended Exercises

Most general calisthenics are good for tennis players. The trick is to select a mix that you'll enjoy doing and that will benefit all the muscle groups equally. More and more players today —myself included—have been working with weights as a means of increasing strength. You can work with light weights—five- and ten-pound dumbweights—on your own, but if you want to work with the heavier weights, you should get some professional instruction. Most Y's have weight-training rooms and instructors to get you started.

HAND AND WRIST. You need both a strong grip and a strong wrist to play tennis well. Any number of inexpensive gadgets designed to strengthen each can be found in sporting goods stores and many tennis pro shops. Keep such aids handy. Work with them when you're just sitting around at home reading or watching television. Squeezing a tennis ball or squash ball is also good exercise.

STOMACH. Stomach muscles play a far more important role to good tennis than you may think. All the bending and stretching you do in a typical match puts a tremendous amount of pressure on your stomach muscles. Strong stomach muscles help you run better too. The weaker your stomach muscles are, the sooner you get fatigued and the more strain you're going to put on your back. Many of the players with back problems do special stomach exercises as therapy, the idea being that with stomach muscles strong enough, the back won't be under as much strain. Sit-ups are excellent stomach conditioners. So are the flutter kick exercises described on page 78.

LEG MUSCLES. Jumping rope, of course. Also, toe jumps. You jump as high as you can twenty times, relax and then repeat.

BACK MUSCLES. Like stomach muscles, the muscles of the back can take a beating in tennis, especially on the serve. Several of the professional players—Tom Gorman, Dick Stockton and Manolo Orantes—have back problems so severe they have to exercise regularly. I hesitate to recommend exercises to anybody with a back problem. Check with your doctor or osteopath. If your back is strong and you want to keep it that way, a good exercise is to stand against a wall or door and thrust your pelvis upward so that the small of your back is flat against the wall. Hold that position, relax slowly, and repeat five times.

WIND EXERCISES. Calisthenics don't do much for your wind; the effort isn't sustained enough. Running or jumping rope for sustained periods of time are the most effective stamina builders I know of. Remember to work in the wind sprints. Run full speed for twenty or thirty yards. Stop and walk for twenty, then sprint for another thirty yards.

This final chapter combines technique with strategy. From this point on, the goals I'm going to recommend will be more specific than goals you've been setting for yourself up to now. Each goal you realize will help to make you a more complete tennis player, reducing your areas of weakness and maximizing your areas of strength.

A PERSPECTIVE ON THE GAME

In the final analysis, tennis comes down to a matter of trying to win each point. If you win enough points, you win the game. If you win enough games, you win a set. If you win enough sets, you win the match. But it all begins with each point.

If there were only one way to win a point, we could dismiss the subject of tennis strategy in a single paragraph, but it's not that simple. You can win a point in any number of ways in tennis. You can also lose a point in any number of ways in tennis. Most tennis points, as I'm sure you know, are not *won* but *lost*—lost because of the failure of one player to execute a particular shot at a particular time.

Strategically there are two things that should concern you in tennis. One is how to win points. The other is how to avoid losing points. The easiest way to avoid losing a point on any particular shot is to hit a "safe" return. A "safe" return is any shot in which your chances of missing are relatively slight. A medium-paced forehand aimed so that it lands about five feet from the baseline in the center of the court allows for a much larger margin of error than a fast-paced forehand aimed for the backhand corner. It is a safer shot in the sense that you do not have to hit it precisely the way you intended in order to achieve something very close to what you were trying to do with it.

But is the "safe" shot necessarily the "better" shot in tennis? Here, really, is what tennis strategy is all about. Knowing when to play it "safe" and when to play it not so safe. Knowing when

5
Putting It All Together

to go for a winner and when to simply keep the ball in play. Knowing when to attack and knowing when to defend.

Forgetting for the moment whether or not you have the game to do it, strategic tennis—or, if you want, *percentage tennis*—comes down to which shots work best for certain situations. The true fascination of tennis at the higher levels lies in the fact that the rules that underlie percentage are forever changing. They change according to a tremendous variety of things, including: what sort of a game your opponent is playing, how well your strokes are working, what sort of a surface you are playing on, what the score is—these are just a few of the many questions that enter into the larger question of what constitutes a percentage shot at any given time in the match. It is this larger question that's going to concern us throughout the rest of the book, as we go through individual strokes and specific situations with the purpose of trying to help you get the most out of your game.

A MORE EFFECTIVE SERVE

The serve is the one stroke in tennis in which you are totally in control.

I am assuming, of course, that you can control your serve enough so that first, you are not overly concerned about double faulting, and second, you can hit the ball pretty much where you want it. If you can't do this and if you're still struggling with a second serve, work on technique first, strategy second.

Two decisions face you every time you serve. One is, where do you want to hit the ball? And

two, do you want to put spin on it and, if so, what sort of spin?

Direction

Most instructional books advise you to serve the greater percentage of your serves to the backhand side, especially in doubles. The assumption here is that most club players are weaker from the backhand side than from the forehand side. I don't agree. Yes, among "B" players, serving to the backhand is probably good strategy, but most good players, even at the club level, tend to return more consistently from the backhand side than from the forehand side.

And even if a player does have a great forehand, this doesn't mean that you should constantly avoid it on the serve. Pancho Segura had one of the greatest forehands of all time, but Pancho Gonzales frequently served him wide to the forehand. Gonzales figured that if he could pull Segura wide he could open up the backhand side more and make it more difficult for Segura to run around the backhand and hit his great two-handed forehand. Gonzales also felt it was wrong to completely avoid an opposing player's strength.

All right, you don't serve like Pancho Gonzales, but can still learn a good lesson here. If your opponent has a dangerous shot, and you have a good serve, better to go directly at the power with your best shot. I particularly like a wide slice serve into the deuce court for both singles and doubles.

Of course, if your opponent is blasting back winners off his forehand return, you'd be silly to keep going back for more. Start serving to the other side. Or start following your serve to the net to put on some added pressure. Or, do what Gonzales used to do with pretty good success against Rod Laver: serve the ball right into him.

There are several things you can do when a player has your serve grooved. Take some pace off. Even flip in a couple of meatball serves if you have to. I've sometimes toyed with the idea of serving left-handed just for a change of pace. I can do it. Not well, but well enough to get it in, and I'm sure it would psych out most opponents enough to win the point.

But let's not lose sight of the number one rule of serving: get the ball in. Double faults are a part of tennis, but certainly if you're averaging more than three or four in a match, it's far too many. Each time you double fault, you've really lost more than the point the score shows your opponent now has. You've also lost the edge you had toward winning that point (since you were serving). So a double fault is perhaps closer to a two-point swing than just the loss of one point.

Of course, if you serve aggressively, you have to be prepared for *some* double faults, and if you can throw in three aces for every double fault, it won't hurt you too much. It all comes down, in the end, to how successful you are at getting your first serve in. A good server will get his first serve in seventy-five percent of the time. If your percentage is below this, you're probably serving too hard. Cut down on the pace and spin in some slice serves that clear the net handily, but come down safely into the service box. Your percentage of first serves will get better and so will your percentage of service games won.

I can suggest a couple of other tips that might increase the effectiveness of your serve. The first is take your time between your first and second serves. The tendency among many players—even good players—is to rush the second serve, almost as if they've already made up their minds that they're going to double fault and want to get the whole thing over with very quickly.

The second tip is to avoid the common trap of trying to serve *harder* when your serve isn't working. You would be surprised at the number of good players who fall into this pattern. It's an easy thing to do. You start missing your serves, double faulting, and you get mad. The angrier you get, the harder you press. It's a vicious cycle, and it will stay with you throughout the match until you get hold of yourself, slow down and try to regain a natural serving rhythm.

Knowing the technique of your stroke helps a great deal. On my own serve, for instance, I know that if I let my front hand fall too soon, I'll start hitting the ball into the net.

I'm suggesting two programs here. One should help you develop a stronger second serve. The other should improve your overall serving by improving your ability to control the direction on both your first and second serve.

A BETTER SECOND SERVE

The barriers that prevent many players from developing a better second serve are as much psychological as technical. Some of you are so afraid of double faulting, you refuse to do anything but simply poop the second serve in. You can get away with this strategy in intermediate tennis, but not against a good player. So, to develop a better second service you must be prepared for a while to suffer throughout some double faults. It won't be pleasant. You may find yourself losing because of it. Still, it's a stage you have to go through if you want your second serve to be more effective. You have to learn by experience that hitting a slice serve harder, and with snap, is actually safer than babying it. Only by giving the ball enough top spin to make it dip down in flight can you make such a serve effective.

Solo Drills

Establish a Drilling Sequence That Approximates Game Conditions. A first serve and then a second serve. If you miss the first, hit the second almost as hard as you did the first. At first, set a goal of five consecutive serving sequences without a double fault. If you can't get to five, ease up on the second serve until you can, but *don't ease up too much.* Your goal here is to find a happy balance between a serve you can consistently get in, and a serve that won't invite attack. More important, you want to reach a point at which you're hitting the second serve nearly as hard as the first serve. Strive for depth. Move your grip a little more to the backhand side, and snap the wrist more to impart additional spin to give you an added measure of control. Don't let the ball drop too much. Go after it, catch it high, and let the spin take care of keeping it in the court.

SECOND SERVES ONLY. Once you've established how hard you can hit the second serve with reasonable consistency, practice *only* that serve. Try to hit five in a row, then ten, then fifteen, then twenty. Keep at it. Alternate deuce and ad courts on each serve. Knowing you can hit twenty serves in a row during practice will give you the confidence you need to go for a good second serve in a match.

Game Drills

Once you think you've got a second serve that will stand up under pressure, play sets in which each player has only *one* serve instead of two. This version, incidentally, is an excellent way of reducing the number of double faults you commit in an average match.

Match Play Application

Make up your mind that for six weeks, you're going to reduce the difference in pace that may now exist between your first and second serves. Start with cutting down the pace of your first a little so that you're getting it in at least seventy percent of the time. Then hit your second serve at the pace you've developed in your practice sequences. True, you'll have to be prepared for some double faults, but don't weaken—even on crucial points. That's the true test—to hit your new second serve when the pressure is on. Remember, you're not trying to win matches, only to develop a second serve that's going to win matches for you in the future.

Another good way to develop a second serve under match conditions is to pretend that every serve you hit in a match is a second serve. A social mixed doubles game is often an ideal opportunity to take this approach.

IMPROVING OVERALL SERVING EFFECTIVENESS

Watching Better Players

Next time you watch a professional match in person or on television, take a pencil and paper and make a study of the serving patterns. Keep it simple. Note the score and whether the serve was hit to the forehand side or backhand. See if you can discern a pattern. Then see if later in the match you can predict where a player will serve on a particular point.

Certain players are especially good to watch in this regard. Gonzales was the best. His effectiveness as a server was based on more than his technique. He mixed direction on his serves very effectively. Stan Smith is an intelligent server. So are Dick Stockton and Chris Evert. The point of this charting is to get you to appreciate the thinking that goes into effective serving. Of course, you still have to be able to control the direction of your serves. Here is what we're going to focus on in this six-week program.

Solo Drills

DEVELOPING ACCURACY.   Serving at your normal pace, set up practice sessions in which you're hitting to specific target areas. You should be able to serve the ball to three separate areas of the service box: the forehand corner, the backhand corner and the middle. Start out by trying to hit five consecutive good serves to each area —a solid performance.

ADVANCED ACCURACY.   Use the same general target areas as in the previous drill, but this time see if you can hit consecutive good serves varying the target area after each serve. Start with the forehand target area, move to the center and then to the backhand. When you can go through the sequence at least three times without a miss, you're doing well. If you want to set up a real challenge, set a tennis-ball can in both the forehand and backhand corners. If you can hit either can one out of ten times, you're doing well.

Rallying Drills

PLAY A PREDETERMINED SET.   Play a Set in which every one of your serves must be hit to a predetermined target area (backhand, forehand, center) in order to be counted as good. Count any serve that doesn't land in that area as a fault.

PLAY A VARIED SET.   Play a Set in which you vary the target areas above from game to game: the forehand one game, the backhand the second game, etcetera.

Game Drill

Play a set in which the server must call out the target area he's aiming for before each serve. (Be fair, now. If you're receiving, don't edge over too much to the target side.) The point of this rule is to get you into the habit of serving with some purpose in mind.

Match Play Application

Get into the habit from now on of having an idea, every time you serve, of *where* you want the ball to go. Get to know your opponent's returning patterns. Try to find out which side he likes to hit more aggressively, and on which he's more accurate. Consider playing to his strength, particularly when you're ahead. Learn to mix your serves up, to change target areas. Don't get into a pattern of going for the same serve on the same point in each game. Your opponent will start to anticipate (if he's smart) and before you know it, no matter how well you're serving, he'll have it grooved.

In doubles, start communicating with your partner so that he knows *where* you're going to serve. That way, he'll be in a stronger position to anticipate the return.

IMPROVING YOUR RETURN OF SERVE

Apart from the serve, the return of serve is the only other stroke where you have a little preparatory time to think out some strategy. You're still dependent, of course, on where the serve is hit and how hard, but you know the ball has to land in the box. If you work at it, you can be a lot more prepared than you are now.

Let's not get ahead of ourselves. The number one priority on the return of serve is to get the ball back into play. Anywhere, any way, but into play. Once you can get the ball back consistently, then you can start to think about what you want to do with it.

Let's assume you have enough technical proficiency in your return of service to control its direction against most servers. *Where* you direct the return should depend mainly upon what the server is doing. Is he coming to the net behind the serve? Fine, try to keep the return low. You don't have to blast it back. There's no rule in tennis that says you have to pass the net charger in order to win the point. Let him have the volley, but give him a difficult shot: a low, off-paced shot that he'll have to volley off his shoe tops. The chances are pretty good that he'll miss it, if the return is good enough. But even if he does volley it, it's probably not going to be a strong shot. You should be in a good position to get the ball by him on the next ball.

A low-angled return of serve is especially useful in doubles. One of the more common sequences in good doubles play goes something like this. The serve comes in and is returned well: low and angled. The server has only one option—to volley or half volley up and usually across the center of the net. The returner's partner, meantime, anticipates the return, crosses over and volleys it away for a winner. Everyone applauds the easy putaway even though it was the good low return that set up the winner.

If the server isn't coming to net behind his serve, you don't have to make the return quite so good. In singles, the "safest" return is a crosscourt shot hit two or three feet above the net so that it lands fairly deep. Unfortunately, that "safe" return in doubles is suicide. A good net man will put it away.

How do you deal with the poacher in doubles? Well, everybody has his own method. What I often do when I'm playing doubles is hit my first two or three returns right at the net man. If he volleys them away for winners, that's okay. It's not as if we've lost *our* serve and at least he'll think twice about poaching from now on. But if he misses, he may start to get a little tight and overanxious. Maybe he'll miss a few *other* easy volleys before he gets back his confidence. In any event, it's going to give him something to think about from now on.

Whatever you do, don't let yourself become so intimidated by the poacher that you tighten up and make unnecessary errors. Concentrate on making a good shot, regardless of what the poacher is doing, and accept the fact that occasionally the poacher will hit some spectacular shots. Work the percentages. If he's putting away your crosscourt returns, try to hit a couple of shots down the line. Hit some shots right at him. Take pace off, lob, and don't try to make your returns *too* good. You're not necessarily trying to *win* the point on the return—only to keep the net man "honest."

Another important thing to remember on the return of serve is not to be overly aggressive with it. One of the best pieces of advice that Pancho Segura gave me early in my career was never to overplay the serve, particularly second serves. This advice would serve a lot of intermediates very well. So many times when I watch club players play, I'll see points *lost* on the return of a weak second serve. The problem in nearly every case is that the player returning the serve tries to do too much with the ball. You shouldn't underestimate the difficulty of returning a weak serve. Move in a couple of steps before the serve. If you hit your returns much better off one side than the other, and you have the time, run around the weaker side and go for a good shot. But don't ignore the percentages. You have the time to hit the ball firmly to just about any place you want on some second serves, so don't shave it too fine by aiming too close to the lines. You can attack and still play percentages. Move in on the ball, get it back deep and into one of the corners, and then move in for the volley. Put enough pressure on a player's second serve, and you cut down the effectiveness of his first serve. He'll begin to worry a little bit about missing the first serve, and will probably take some pace off. Against a player with a very good serve, it's difficult to hit consistently strong returns, but this doesn't mean that you can't try different strategies. In the 1976 Aetna World Cup match in Hartford, Arthur Ashe was having trouble with Tony Roche's serve until he started waiting for it about six feet behind the baseline. Standing farther back gave him a little more time to read the spin on the serve and it changed the angle of the return enough so that Roche had trouble with the volley. It helped Arthur win the match.

Six Weeks to a Better Service Return

The return of service is one of the more difficult strokes to improve because you need a cooperative partner to serve you balls on which you can practice. The best way to practice the return is to dovetail your drills with the serving drills (see page 52), letting one player practice the serve while the other practices the return.

Watching Better Players

It's safe to say that the best return of service in tennis today belongs to Jimmy Connors. Still I don't recommend Connors's approach for the average player. There are very few pros, let alone club players, who can hit returns as hard from both sides as Connors and still get them in. The European players and South American players—players who grew up on clay—are good return of service models for the intermediate because they rarely overhit. Nastase, for instance, will almost never go for a winner on his service return. He just concentrates on getting the ball back deep. Pay close attention to where the pros stand when waiting for the serve. Against certain servers, I've seen some players stand three or four feet behind the baseline waiting for the first serve. It goes back to

what I said much earlier—that the chief priority is to get the ball back.

Watch how the good players vary their returns. Laver can be just as effective when he chips his backhand return at a sharp angle as when he blasts the ball back. Newcombe will often wait for the second serve shifted all the way around to the forehand side, advertising the fact that he's going to attack with his forehand. It unnerves some players. Ashe has a lot of variety in the way he returns, too. It's made him a much better player over the past couple of years.

Rallying Drills

FOREHAND AND BACKHAND CONTROL. Have your practice partner serve ten consecutive times to you on one side, and then ten to the other, until you've handled one hundred. Practice different *types* of returns. In one sequence try to return the ball deep. In another sequence, try to keep the ball low and shallow. Work for variety on both sides.

RETURNING HARD SERVES. If you know a very good server at your club or park who likes to practice his serve frequently, ask if you can practice returns off it. Most players are happy to have somebody return their serves. It approximates game conditions more, and means less running after and gathering up balls.

SECOND SERVE CONTROL. Practice returning your partner's more aggressive second serves. Develop your ability to hit forcing returns off either side. The forehand return from the ad court into the forehand corner of your opponent is a good attacking return of second serve. Work on moving to the net behind deep second serve returns.

MOVING IN. Stand two or three feet inside the baseline to return practice serves against a partner who doesn't have a particularly strong serve. Standing closer will give you less time to react and should approximate match conditions when you're playing against a player with a fast serve. Practice blocking the ball back.

Game Drills

ONE-SIDE RETURN OF SERVE. Play a set in which you try to return as many serves as you can from only one side. To hit backhand returns (if you're right-handed), edge over toward your right more, leaving a lot of open area down the center. To hit forehand returns, edge over toward the other side.

TARGET SERVICE RETURN. Play a set in which the service return must be hit to a certain place on the court if the point is going to count. Vary the target areas from game to game. In one game, count only crosscourt returns (backhand or forehand) as good. In another, make only low shallow returns count as good.

Match Play Application

Try over the next six weeks to play against the strongest servers you know. In each set, work on one particular return more than others. For example, hit only short angled returns for one set, concentrating on either backhand or forehand. In another set, make up your mind simply to get the ball back deep. Develop the confidence to meet more aggressive second serves by moving in and taking the ball early.

IMPROVING YOUR DEFENSIVE GAME

The complete tennis player knows how to defend and how to attack. More important, he knows when to use each strategy. If I were to establish priorities, I'd place the ability to play defensively over the ability to attack, certainly in club tennis. There are very few players, even among the pros, who can play attacking tennis all the time and not make so many errors that they end up beating themselves. There are practically no players outside of pro ranks who can hit the ball hard consistently and not make more errors then winners. The keys to a better defensive game are steadiness and patience, and your goals during any six-week period in which you want to improve your defensive tennis should be keyed to each of these things.

Watching Better Players

There are many professional players on the circuit today whose games are built primarily around defense. They include Chris Evert, Harold Solomon, Guillermo Vilas and Björn Borg. Whether or not you like the styles of these particular players, you can learn a lot from them and would do well to incorporate into your own game certain elements they represent.

Chris Evert is an especially good model. She illustrates how effective just two things, consistency and depth, can be. Seldom do any of her ground strokes land shallow unless she deliberately puts the ball there. She knows she can keep the ball in play longer than just about anybody she plays, so the pressure is always on the other player to do something *more*. That something more is just as likely to produce an error as it is a winning point.

Harold Solomon also illustrates the benefits of patience and consistency. Nobody, least of all Harold himself, would deny that Harold would be a much better player if he could pressure his opponents a little more from the net. But he's done very well over the past couple of years even without possessing too much of a net game. Solomon comes to every match knowing that in order to win, he's going to be on the court for at least an hour longer than players who play a more attacking game. He has patience, he very seldom errs from the backcourt, and he's in great shape. He also has the ability to pass well on either side. His strategy is simple. If you want to beat him, you have to do it from the net, which means you come to his strength —his passing shots. What's more, until you can get the right shot to approach behind, you have to be prepared to sit tight on the baseline, meanwhile never making an error. Many of the top players today, who've always played an attacking brand of tennis, simply don't have the patience to wait, and that's when they play right into Harold's hands.

To repeat what I said earlier: I don't necessarily recommend that you model your game after Solomon's or Chris Evert's. It may fit your talents and personality, and it may not. Even so, you should learn to appreciate the effectiveness of these elements and be able to incorporate them to some degree into your own game.

Rallying Drills (steadiness)

KEEPING THE BALL IN PLAY. Structure your practice sessions with this goal in mind: keeping the ball in play. Start out at the baseline and work from one side at a time, forehand and backhand. Set an initial goal of six consecutive good balls, never allowing any ball to bounce more than once. Once you can reach six, raise the total to eight, then ten, twelve, until you can consistently keep the ball in play an average of fifteen consecutive times without a miss.

Game Drill

Play a set with the following rules. In the first two games, no point can be won by either player unless the ball has been kept in play at least four times, with the serve and return of serve counting as one each. If an error occurs before the ball has gone over and back four times, play a point as a let. In the next two games, raise the minimum total to six, and continue raising it every two games until you reach twelve. There will be times during these games, obviously, when one of you will have an easy putaway but won't attempt to hit the shot because the minimum hasn't been met. Don't worry. The purpose of playing with these rules is not to win games, but to get you to develop more patience and consistency.

Match Play Application

Over the next six weeks, concentrate, above all, on keeping the ball in play. Except in the most obvious situations, resist the temptation to win the point outright. If this is hard for you, tell yourself you're going to keep the ball in play for at least four or five returns before looking to attack. The interesting thing you may discover if you employ this strategy is that simply by keeping the ball in play longer, the attacking strategy becomes unnecessary because your opponent has meanwhile made an error.

IMPROVING CONTROL

Once you've developed an element of steadiness into your defensive game, you're ready to start working on control: being able not only to keep the ball in play, but hitting to specific areas.

Solo Drills

BOUNCE AND HIT (DEPTH). Take a basket of balls out with you to the baseline. Bounce and hit backhands and forehands, striving for depth. Set an initial goal of ten consecutive forehands or backhands that land beyond the service line.

BOUNCE AND HIT (DIRECTION). Add a target area dimension to the preceding drill. Stand initially in the forehand corner of the deuce court. Try to hit ten consecutive good shots across the court beyond the service line and then down the line beyond the service line. Move to the other side and work in the same way on the backhand.

MORE BOUNCE AND HIT (DIRECTION). Take the basket with you to various areas of the court and practice hitting from these areas to specific areas on the other side of the net. Again set goals for yourself. Try to hit at least ten in a row.

Rallying Drills

DEPTH. Practice backhands and forehands from the baseline, striving to hit the ball deep enough so that it lands beyond the service line every time. It will probably mean hitting the ball higher over the net and not hitting it quite so hard. Set an initial goal of six in a row off each side, forehand and backhand, and work up to twelve.

DIRECTION. Practice baseline forehands and backhands with specific target areas. Work on these four in particular: From the deuce corner: down the line and crosscourt; from the ad corner: down the line and crosscourt. Establish an initial goal of six consecutive good shots. Work up to twelve. The ability to execute these shots from these areas is the basis of a sound passing game.

DIRECTION (ADVANCED). Establish target areas approximately four feet by four feet in each corner of the singles court. See how many times in a row you can hit ground strokes that hit the target, stroking from various points along the sidelines.

PASSING SHOT PRACTICE. Here's an excellent practice drill for developing variety and consistency in your passing shots. You and your practice partner line up opposite each other at your respective baselines. Your partner simulates an approach shot, bouncing the ball and hitting it to your forehand or backhand. He then moves up into the net position. Your job is to hit a passing shot. Work on specific shots one at a time. Start with a forehand down the line. Then work on forehand crosscourt, backhand down the line, backhand crosscourt. Finally, practice low shots aimed for the net man's feet. You can set goals here, too. Or, you can keep a running score of how many successful and unsuccessful passing shots you hit. Meanwhile, your practice partner is working on his volleys.

LOBBING DRILLS. Follow the procedure described in the previous drill, but this time hit lobs instead of passing shots. Work on forehands and backhand lobs and, in each case, set a target area. Your practice partner can work on his overhead while you practice depth and direction on your lob. This is a valuable drill. As I said earlier, the reason most players don't lob well is that they don't practice the shot enough.

PASSING SHOTS AND LOBS. Combine the last two drills by alternating passing shots with lobs. A workable sequence might be as follows: (1) forehand down the line passing shot; (2) forehand lob down the line; (3) forehand off-pace low shot aimed at feet of net man; (4) forehand lob crosscourt. Now reverse things and try doing it all off backhand shots.

Game Drills

DEPTH. Play sets in which any ground stroke landing within the service line is "out." Since height over the net is the key to depth, you might add this condition: that any ball that goes into the net loses you *two* points not one.

DIRECTION. Play sets in which you establish various target areas. For example, in order for a return to be considered "good" in one game it should land in the portion of the deuce court beyond the service line. This means that every shot you hit, forehand or backhand, has to be hit to that spot. Set a similar condition for your opponent. A variation of this drill is to set restrictions on what you can do with each shot. You might play a game in which every forehand you hit has to be hit crosscourt, etcetera. Games like these are invaluable for building into your game the control that characterizes good players, because they force you to make specific shots.

Match Play Application

Each time you go out to play a match over the next six weeks, work on one particular aspect of defensive tennis. Decide, for instance, that you will hit every one of your backhand passing shots down the line, regardless of where your opponent is. On another day, work solely on hitting low balls that force defensive volleys. Each match focuses on some specific part of the defensive game, allowing that part of your game to be tested under match conditions. On a more basic level, make up your mind to hit as many crosscourt forehands or backhands as you can, or to simply play a totally defensive strategy —one in which your only goal is to keep the ball in play, but hitting to specific spots on the opposing court.

While you're approaching the game in this way, don't make the mistake of confusing *defensive* tennis with *tentative* tennis. A strictly defensive game won't work against good players unless you're willing to go for your shots when they come up. This applies, in particular, to your passing shots. You can't get away with just easing the ball back when you're under pressure from a good player at the net. Take a full stroke—not necessarily a hard swing, but one in which you're hitting *through* the ball. Fight the tendency when you're under pressure to rush your stroke. Sometimes you have no choice, but often you have more time than you think—providing you move quickly and get ready early. No matter where you turn in tennis, it always comes down to the same thing: fundamentals.

BUILDING ATTACK INTO YOUR GAME

With enough quickness, enough stamina and enough control over the basic strokes, you should be able to compete in upper levels of club tennis wherever you go, but if your game lacks an attacking dimension, its ultimate growth will be limited. I said it earlier: the complete tennis player—relative to any level—is the player who can defend *and* attack. Other things being equal, a player who can defend and not attack will usually beat the player who can attack but not defend, the reason being that the percentages—in club tennis, at any rate—nearly always favor the steadier player. But by not incorporating some element of attack into your game you're not only short-circuiting your potential, you're missing out on much of the enjoyment tennis has to offer.

The key to the attacking or forcing game is knowing *when* to attack: on which balls, on which points, and at which stage in the match. There's as much of a percentage element in the attacking game as there is in the defensive game. Unless you respect these percentages, it's hard to win.

To play an attacking game you have to be able to do a number of things well. First, you have to be able to serve well. Secondly, you have to move well and react quickly. And, finally, you need a dependable volley. Notice, I said "dependable" volley. You don't need to be a spectacular volleyer to be effective as long as you hit your approach shots well enough and move into position quickly enough.

Hitting Better Approach Shots

A lot of intermediate tennis players take approach shots for granted. You shouldn't. There are techniques and strategies that relate specifically to approach shots, and the success of an attacking game depends to a large extent on how well you understand and are able to execute them.

The ability to hit effective approach shots begins with knowing which shots to approach behind. A common mistake among intermediate players is to try for an approach shot off a return that has been hit deep into his own court. Hitting approach shots off the balls that land deep in your own court is inadvisable for two reasons: (1) the percentages of hitting a forcing shot from deep in your backcourt are not favorable; (2) you're usually too far from the net to get into a strong volleying position.

As a general rule, you should only try to come to net behind a strong serve, or behind an approach shot that you've made from a spot fairly shallow in your court—say, around the service line. Once you see a ball is going to land shallow, you move up to it quickly, *making sure your racket is back* as you move to the ball. If possible, you want to make contact with the ball on approach shots at or near the top of the bounce. The lower the ball is when you make contact, the more difficult it is to control the direction and/or pace of the ball.

You don't have to hit an approach shot too hard. Remember, you're not trying to win the point outright on that shot, only to set yourself up for a winning volley. Hit a good shot but, above all, a safe shot. More important than pace is depth and placement. You don't have to take a full stroke on the approach shot. The technique I recommend is almost, but not quite, like a volley. You're moving into the ball and spotting it to where you want it to go. Underspin is good on an approach shot if you can hit it with control, because an underspin shot will stay low when it bounces and give your opponent a more difficult passing shot.

Where do you aim your approach shots? The general rule is to hit toward your opponent's weaker side—the side from which his passing shots are less effective. That's not an ironclad rule, and I think it's better to vary your approach shots.

It's not a bad idea, for instance, to hit an occasional approach shot right at the opposing player, in the center of the court. Hitting the ball down the center cuts down a little on the passing shots angles open to your opponent, but that stratagem works better against certain players than others.

Placing the Volley

Assuming you've hit a good approach shot, the next question is where you try to guide your volley. It's simply a matter of where you and your opponent happen to be. The main thing is not to overdo it. Most intermediates tend to overhit volleys the same way they overhit ground strokes. There's no rule that says you have to win the point on your first volley. A lot of the top players—Stan Smith and Roscoe Tanner, in particular—use the first volley to pull the other player out of position, the better to produce a weak passing shot from him that you can more easily put away.

Placing the Overhead

If you play an attacking game, you must be prepared to deal with the lob. This means being able to hit the overhead with some consistency. Like the volley, the overhead does not have to be hit hard in order for it to be a winner. If you can place it to either side, you can win the point just as easily as if you pound the ball so hard that it bounces out of the court. Respect good lobs. If the ball is hit very high, let it bounce first. If it gets behind you, get back quickly and hit a safe shot back. I can't emphasize this point too much. A successful attacking strategy is built around the ability to know when to attack and when not to attack.

Hitting Winners

I have been stressing the importance of keeping the ball in play, of keeping the pressure on the other player so that he is more likely to make the error than you are. I'm not going to change this advice, but there are occasions when you have to go for winners. Often I see two club players in the midst of a rally, and one of the players will have an open court: an easy chance to win the point. And what happens? He plays it so safely that his opponent runs down the ball and keeps the rally alive.

It happens all the time in doubles too, at the club level. A server puts in a good serve. The return is weak, and the server's partner moves across at net to take the ball. And then—for no reason—he sends the ball back without any attacking purpose. What usually happens is that a point that should have been in the bag is lost —a swing of two points!

My advice in this regard is short and quick. If you have an opening, take advantage of it. I don't mean wind up and pound the ball with everything you have. It's not necessary. Just don't tighten up. Many players have trouble with the "sitter"—the ball that is just waiting there to be put away. What happens on these shots, I suspect, is that players tend to think about them a little too much. Relax. Hit the ball the way you normally would, but go for a winner.

If you constantly miss easy shots that you should be putting away, there's a good chance that you're rushing. It's understandable, but correctable. Don't be overanxious. If the other player is out of position, don't *you* hurry to hit the shot. Don't take any *more* time than you need, but don't take any less time either. Also, try to hit the ball as close to the top of the bounce as possible. The secret to hitting put-aways is meeting the ball high and swinging down.

SIX WEEKS TO A MORE ATTACKING GAME

The main thing you have to remember about building elements of attack into your tennis game is that you don't necessarily have to increase the power in your strokes. A strategy based on attack is pointless if you give away as many points as you win. Learn to recognize situations in a match that call for offensive strategy. Develop skills that will support an attacking game, in particular a good overhead and a steady volley. Improve your quickness and your serve. Both are indispensable to a genuine offensive strategy. For a while you must be prepared to make more errors than you normally do.

The chief reason for adding an extra attacking dimension to your game is that as you move into the higher plateaus of tennis, you will often meet a player who is as steady or steadier than you and who can only be beaten if you can attack. The more variety you can bring to the tennis court, the more complete player you're going to be. Solid play remains the basis of a sound game, but you need something *more* to advance to higher levels of tennis.

Watching Better Players

The players that come to my mind most readily when I think about "aggressive" tennis are Rod Laver, Arthur Ashe, and Jimmy Connors. What's interesting to watch about Laver and Ashe is their ability to mix up their power with some soft stuff. They prove the point I stressed earlier: that offensive tennis isn't built on power alone. Watch how they hit their approach shots, especially Ashe. Arthur will miss an occasional volley, but he rarely makes an error on his approach. When watching Connors, note how high he meets the ball when he's attacking.

Solo Drills

SERVE AND VOLLEY. When you practice your serve, move up toward the net each time. If you are going to learn to volley the return, you've got to learn to get into position. Strive for smoothness in your motion, and a well-balanced

position when you finish up. Make sure you don't foot fault, but you should be already moving forward by the time the racket finishes its downward arc.

HITTING WINNERS FROM THE FORECOURT. Take a basket of balls and bounce and hit them from various areas of the forecourt. Hit them from both sides as if you were going for a winning placement. Get a feel for how hard you have to hit the ball to keep it in the court. Practice some angled top-spin shots from the same place.

Rallying Drills

SERVE AND VOLLEY. Being able to come in behind your serve isn't an absolute prerequisite for winning singles on the club level, but it's vital in high level doubles. Even if you don't intend to play the serve and volley game in singles, it doesn't hurt at all to be able to do it now and then as a way of preventing your opponent from getting into a groove on his return. Serve and volley drills are best done when the receiver, instead of hitting the serve back, lets it go and hits a ball from his hand that the server has to volley. Practicing serve and volley in this way allows the returner to put the ball wherever he wants to, thereby giving the server more opportunities to hit volleys from different places on the court. Give special attention to the low volley made off a soft low return. It's one of the toughest shots in tennis.

APPROACH SHOT AND VOLLEY. Rally from the baseline but with the idea that anytime either of you hits a ball that lands near the service line the other player will move up, hit an approach shot and then try to win the point on a volley or overhead. The player under attack can respond with either a passing shot or a lob.

FOUR-BALL DRILL. You serve to a receiver who holds four balls in his hand, or if he can't, tucks one or two in a pocket. The receiver disregards the serve, but regardless of whether it goes in or not you follow it to the net. The receiver bounce/hits one of the balls in his hand to your forehand side for one volley, then immediately bounce/hits a ball to your backhand side for a volley, then hits up a lob to one side, and then a lob to the other. When you can consistently hit four good shots in a row in this drill, you should be able to play an attacking game with reasonable success.

ADVANCED VOLLEYING. Station yourself at the net, a basket of balls close at hand, with your partner at his baseline. His job is to mix up shots, hitting some wide to your right, some wide to your left, and some directly at you. Don't try to do much with the shots you really have to stretch for. Block them back nice and deep, and get back quickly into position. Work on placement.

TWO-ON-ONE DRILLS. The best way to develop proficiency at the net is to set two of your practice partners at the baseline with a basket of balls and have them pelt you with a barrage of ground strokes, lobs and drop shots. Stay on your toes. Getting into good position before you hit is all-important.

FORECOURT DRILLS. Have your practice partner hit, out of his hand, balls that bounce fairly high inside the service line. Your job is to move in and put the ball away. Work from both sides, and direct your shots to various spots on the other side of the court. Try to get to the ball early and meet it high so that you have a safe angle to work from. Hit the ball solidly, but don't overhit. Let the racket head do the work.

Game Drills

FOLLOW SERVES TO THE NET. Play a set in which you must follow every one of your serves to the net. Make the same rule for both players in order to even things up.

POINT RESTRICTIONS. Play a set in which a point is won only when it is produced by a clean winner or by a shot so strong that it brings on an error. (Here, for once, I'm not interested in the number of errors you make. I just want you to get the feel of going for your shots.)

MEET GROUND STROKES AT NET. Play a set in

which you *must* come to net on any ground stroke that doesn't land beyond the service line. Otherwise you lose the point.

Match Play Application

Start to play more aggressively! That's all I have to say, really, in the way of advising you on how to develop an attacking game. Not recklessly, just more aggressively. Make up your mind to follow at least two, maybe three, of your first serves to the net every game you play, regardless of your opponent and regardless of the score. You'll have time later to be more selective about when you do this. On *any* shallow ball, move in, hit the approach shot and try to end the point with one or two volleys. *Think* aggressively. Be on the lookout for opportunities for attacking. Anytime you get a high short ball in the forecourt, go for the winner. There's a direct correlation between your confidence and how successfully you can incorporate aggressive strategy into your game, but you'll never build up your confidence unless you execute the strokes enough times under match conditions.

Mental Toughness and How to Improve It

How frequently do you play matches in which you perform at a level you consider very close to, if not at the height of, your potential at this stage of your game? Do you hit the ball as well in a match as you do in practice? How frequently are you so intimidated by the other player or by conditions to a point that you simply cannot play your best? How much of a problem are nerves for you on a tennis court?

Answering these questions takes us into a category known as "mental toughness." Mental toughness, as I see it, is the ability to prevent factors not *directly* related to hitting the ball from getting in the way of your performance. It is more difficult to develop mental toughness than it is to develop the technical aspects of your game. I can teach you how to hit a technically sound serve, and I can teach you how to use that technically sound serve to strategic advantage. I *can't* teach you the mental toughness that will enable you to combine these two things successfully at critical points in the match.

Being "mentally tough" doesn't mean that you never get nervous or never "choke" on big points in a match. I've never met a good player in my life who wasn't affected to some degree by nerves, and by the mental pressure of tennis. The *real* question is how much and how often do these pressures affect your play. Numerous factors determine the answer to this question, but the three that strike me as being the most important are (1) the desire to win; (2) confidence; (3) concentration.

The Desire to Win

I doubt if there has ever been a truly successful competitor in any sport who was not motivated by a tremendous desire to win. I'm not interested in judging whether it's good or bad to feel this way. I'm simply saying that you have to bring more to the competitive situation than technique if you hope to be successful.

I have always gone into each competition I've ever been involved in with the idea of winning, and even though I'm better about it today than I've ever been, I still have difficulty accepting

defeat. One thing I've learned to do is to react more to my own performance than to the outcome of the match. That means that, if I lose but played well, I don't get down on myself. I've also learned to give the other player credit, something I didn't always do in the past.

I've met tennis players at different levels of the game who have said to me that winning is unimportant to them. I have no reason to doubt their word. Then again, I wonder if they might not be using this attitude as an excuse. I've worked with recreational players who began with this attitude but who changed the minute their games started to get a little better.

By the same token, I've met players so consumed by winning they were willing to do just about anything, even cheat, if the outcome of a match might be affected. I feel sorry for people like this. I make a clear distinction between going out on the court and playing your heart out to win, and going out on the court with the idea that you'll do *anything* to win.

Obviously, there's a balance here. I see nothing wrong with playing to win, and I can understand a player being down when he loses. But there are limits. If the only way you can win is to bend the rules and to do things deliberately calculated to upset your opponent, you're not going to win my respect no matter how many tennis trophies you accumulate. And, if you're still down in the mouth the day after you've lost a match, I think you should take a good hard look at yourself to get your priorities back in line again. I've had some big wins in my career, and I have had some very bitter losses. It's more pleasant for me to recall the wins than to look back upon the losses, but I can honestly say that the losses, tough though they may be, have helped me. Defeat can either break your spirit or make you stronger and determined to do better the next time.

Confidence

Nothing is more elusive in tennis than confidence. Your confidence can vary from month to month, week to week, day to day, and even from moment to moment in a match. I can recall matches in my own career, where in the space of maybe ten to fifteen minutes, I've gone from playing miserable tennis, convinced I didn't stand a chance in the match, to playing nearly perfect tennis at the end. In 1970, when I beat Rod Laver at Forest Hills, I lost five of the first six games and at 5–1, with Laver serving, I began to wonder if I was going to win another game in the match. What happened was that I said to myself, the heck with it, and I started to hit the ball. I broke serve—and eventually won the set. That gave me the confidence I needed to play well the rest of the match. The next day, when I played against Cliff Richey, my confidence somehow was gone, and I lost.

Elusive as confidence is, there are some definite things you can do, I believe, to increase your level of confidence before you go into a match. What you do to get ready for a match, for instance, can go a long way to affect your confidence. Here's where training and physical conditioning assume so much importance. If you can come into a match feeling sharp and alert, knowing that you can run for a couple of hours if necessary and not get tired, you're going to be a lot more confident than you'd be if you had gone out on the court having had only three or four hours' sleep the night before. Again, I'm not telling you how to live your life, only that doing your best on a tennis court carries with it certain prerequisites of life-style.

Knowing something about your opponent helps. For the good professional player, tennis is a twenty-four-hour-a-day job. You may be playing somebody who is technically better than you, but if you can exploit his weakness successfully you can minimize the differences between you and possibly go on to win. It's not always possible, of course. It may be you simply don't have the shots you need in order to exploit a particular weakness. Still, simply knowing what you have to do—having a plan—gives you a certain amount of confidence.

The best way to find out about an opponent is to watch him play some matches. See what he likes to do with his serve. See if he has a second serve you can attack. Watch to see if he likes to lob, and pay attention to what he does with his passing shots. Most players favor certain passing shots over others, and knowing whether your opponent is more likely to go down the line or go crosscourt is a valuable piece of information.

If you don't get a chance to see your opponent play, you have to rely on your warm-up. The warm-up is a time when you should be thinking about your own strokes, but you can watch the other player, too. See whether he's more forceful off the forehand than backhand, and by how much. Test his overhead and volleys. If your opponent chooses not to hit volleys or overheads in the warm-up, there's a good chance he's weak in these areas, and so you have something to work with.

Follow this advice, but don't lose sight of your own game. You should know pretty much what you can and what you can't accomplish on a court, and if you can make up your mind to stay within your game, as much as possible, you'll probably do better than a stronger player who is constantly trying things that are beyond his capabilities.

At the beginning of the match, try not to *give* way any points. Play solid, sensible tennis. Giving away points is never good policy.

Keep the pressure on the other player in the beginning. Let him make the mistakes. One of the things I recommend to players I've coached in pressure situations is to start the match by simply trying to keep ground strokes fairly deep but in a more or less central zone on the other side of the court—shots, in other words, with a safe margin of error. Once you've developed some rhythm on *these* shots, then you can start going for the lines more.

This technique, of altering your target zones, can be used throughout the match. If you find yourself giving away points with unforced errors, go back to the strategy you used at the beginning. Hit good shots but safe shots. Get your rhythm and confidence back. *Then* start to try more. Remember, nothing is worse for your confidence than unforced errors. Keep them down to the barest minimum, especially at the start of the match, and your level of confidence in a match should increase as the match draws on.

Concentration

Nobody reading this book needs to be reminded about the importance of good concentration to good tennis. However, the question is whether I, or anybody, can teach you to concentrate.

I don't think so. I can stress the value of it and talk about some of the techniques I've used, but concentration is something each player has to train himself or force himself to do in his own way.

It can be done. You have to practice concentration just the same way you work on your serve or volley. I see many players at all levels missing shots and losing matches for no other reason than poor concentration or lapses in concentration. It's an easy thing to let happen. You let noises distract you. You let the wind bother you. You let people in other courts or in the stands disturb you. You fume over what you

think is a bad call against you. It's easy to blame these things for your errors, but they are just excuses for your inability to concentrate. The top players never let anything interfere with their concentration. Anything.

From my own experience, I can tell you that lapses of concentration are the most likely to occur when you're not really enjoying the game, that is, when you'd rather be someplace else. I'm not making excuses, but one of the main reasons that I sometimes lost concentration in a match when I was younger is that I didn't like the idea of being so far away from my family. Some of the pros who are married and have children are able to put everything else out of their minds when they get out on the court. I can do this some of the time, but I can remember tournaments abroad where I would be toweling off in between games and instead of thinking about the match, I'd be thinking about my wife and kids thousands of miles away. "What in the world am I *doing* here?" I can remember asking myself, and if I remember correctly, those were the matches I usually lost.

The big problem in concentration isn't so much thinking *about* the game, it's not letting other things interfere. In other words, blocking out everything but the game. It takes practice to do this, and that's why the players who work on concentration during practice concentrate well during a game.

Concentration is much tougher for club players than it is for the pros. You're a young mother and you've packed off three kids to school, and now you're running to get to your indoor game in between errands, and you try to focus on tennis for an hour or an hour and a half, and it doesn't work. Your mind is a hundred other places.

Nevertheless, I don't care who you are, you can still do a better job of concentrating. Start with the warm-up. Watch the ball all the way to the racket. *Listen* (yes, listen) to the ball as it comes off the racket. If there's an interesting game going on in the next court, ignore it. If there's commotion outside the court—some kids running around or something—pay no attention.

A second thing that might help you concentrate better in a match is to start out with the idea that for the first few points, all you want to do is to keep the ball in play, to establish a playing rhythm. Most players start running into concentration problems the minute they start to miss. You immediately start looking around for excuses: the sun, the lighting, the surface, the noise. So you hit a couple of shots long, or into the net. Forget about it. Get your balance, get back into position, and relax. If you've missed a couple of easy shots in a game, forget them. The points are gone. You'll never get them back. Concentrate on the next one.

After each game, though, you can focus in a little on what you might be doing wrong. Keep it simple. Check your balance, and eye contact. And think about one point at a time. Remember, if you're down love–30, you still only need two points to be even. Play each point one at a time and you may win four in a row.

Late in a match, you might get a little tired, and that can have an effect on concentration, too. What has always helped me when I'm tired is to say to myself, "Well, if I'm pooped he's got to be tired too." Instead of saying to yourself, "Oh, no. Here it is only the very beginning of the third set and already I'm exhausted," say something like, "Okay, if I really focus in, I can finish this thing off in twenty minutes, and I'll have plenty of time to rest afterward." Set little goals. At the start of a game, say to yourself, "I just have to win four points." Then, as you win a point, "Three to go," and so forth.

Above all, keep your cool. I may not be the ideal player who comes to mind when you think about controlling temper on the court, but I don't feel as if I got any angrier than most of my fellow players when I was younger. I *did* get written up about it more.

Still, I admit that almost every time I got angry, it cost me. The tendency when you get angry is to blast, to let off steam, and that's when you start making errors, losing confidence and losing concentration. I'll never forget a Davis Cup match against Australia in Cleveland. I was playing Fred Stolle, and I was ahead, but it was a very hot day, and I was getting very tired and was extremely thirsty. The Australian team had a big bucket of oranges in ice, and all we had were some warm Cokes standing in the dirt.

I blew up. I shouldn't have, but I did, and it cost me the match. I like to think the same thing wouldn't happen today. The minute you feel yourself getting upset, you have to remind yourself that the only person you're hurting by getting angry is yourself. Anger only produces sloppier play and saps your energy. In the end, it's your opponent who will benefit. I speak from experience.

In Chapter 1, I talked about testing yourself as a good way to help establish an improvement strategy. Here is a testing routine designed to measure your technical proficiency based on the 20-in-a-Row standard I wrote about. Don't expect to score a "20" in every situation, or even come close in some instances. What we're looking for is the number of times, on the average, between 0 and 20 that you can execute a particular stroke in a particular situation.

To take these tests, you will need either a cooperative partner or a ball machine. If you use a partner, try to get somebody who can control his strokes sufficiently to give you enough hits by which to get a score. Your partner can either hit balls out of his hand on one bounce, or else keep the rally going. In any event, the only thing you're measuring is *your* number of consecutive hits. If your partner, or the ball machine, hits an out ball, disregard it and proceed with the test from the point at which the error occurred.

The balls you hit should come to you at a medium pace and should be hit reasonably close to you. You can disregard any ball that presents you with an unusually difficult return, but don't be too easy on yourself. The more you can simulate match conditions (within reason), the more valid, and valuable, will be the overall barometer of your technical proficiency.

Another thing. Don't just poop the ball over the net. To get an accurate picture of your strengths and weaknesses, you should hit the ball pretty much the way you do when you play a match. We're not handing out any prizes for the best score, so there's no purpose at all in holding back. You'll only be kidding yourself.

HOW TO SCORE

To simply go out on a one-shot basis and test yourself in a particular stroke situation isn't going to tell you very much. That's why our aim in these tests is to come up with an *average* figure. To come up with a reasonably accurate average,

I recommend that you complete no less than five testing situations (you can do as many as you like, if you want to) for each stroke. By sequence, I'm talking about the number of times you hit a particular shot without a miss, up to 20. Any shot you fail to hit back or that lands out constitutes an end to that sequence at the number of your last "good" shot.

To make things a little easier for you, I'll let you disregard your lowest score in the sequence. So, assuming you've completed five sequences, you would compute your average by adding up the four highest totals and then by dividing that figure by four. If you were to hit 20 each time, your average, of course, would be 20, and I'll be looking for you next summer at Forest Hills. Otherwise, if your scores ran, 12, 8, 10, 3, and 6, your total, tossing out the 3, would be 36. Divide by 4 and you'd get 9.

THE TESTING PROCEDURE

Forehand Drive

Determine the average number of consecutive times you can keep the ball in play when hitting forehands under the following conditions.

No Special Target Area. Station yourself in the center of the court along the baseline. Count as "good" any ball that lands within the singles boundaries on the other side.

Crosscourt. Station yourself a foot or so to the left of the singles sideline in the deuce court (other side of the court for lefties) and count as "good" only those balls that clear the net and land in the deuce court on the other side (the ad court for lefties).

Down the Line. Station yourself a few feet to the right of the center mark on the baseline, and count as "good" only those balls that land in the ad court on the other side.

Backhand Drive

Go through the same three sequences on your backhand drive as you did in the preceding forehand sequences. Obviously the sides you hit from, and into, on the crosscourt and down-the-line sequences will be the reverse of those used when you were testing your forehand drive.

Volleying

Assume a position about a yard inside the service line, straddling the line that separates the two service boxes. Have your partner hit balls to you at a reasonable pace. Disregard any chances that are especially difficult.

Forehand Volley

Determine the average number of times you can keep a forehand volley in play in the following situations.

1. With no Special Target Area.
2. Into the deuce court.
3. Into the ad court.

Backhand Volley

(Follow same sequence as forehand volley.)

Serving

Test the consistency of your serve with the following conditions:

1. Serve at the pace you normally use for your second serve. Alternate serves into ad and deuce courts. Count as "good" any good serve.

2. Aim for specific target areas, starting in the deuce court, aiming first to forehand and then to backhand side. If you get both in, move to other side and repeat procedure. If you don't get both in, stay in the same court until you do. Follow this alternating pattern throughout the test.

The Lob

The best way to take the lob test is to have your partner stand at the net feeding you balls from either his hand or his racket. In order for a lob to be counted "good," it must land beyond the service line. Test under the following conditions.

1. Forehand crosscourt
2. Backhand crosscourt
3. Forehand down the line
4. Backhand down the line

Overheads

Overheads are difficult to test, but do your best anyway. Take the volleying position. Have your partner hit you fairly high lobs that would land somewhere around the service line if allowed to bounce. Hit smashes only off your forehand. The conditions:

1. No special target area
2. Into the deuce court
3. Into the ad court

FINDING OUT MORE ABOUT YOUR GAME

If you've taken the tests described above, you should have a fair idea of your basic technical proficiency in various phases of the game. Some of the sequences—those where there's no particular target area—are easier than the others, and any even fairly decent intermediate should average at least ten on these, and not be content until he or she can score pretty close to a perfect twenty. On the more difficult sequences, involving placement and touch, scores will vary all over the lot. Since you can throw out your poorest performance in calculating your average, I'd say you ought to be able to put together something like five or six in a row on each of these sequences, if you think of yourself as any sort of a respectable intermediate, and shouldn't start to feel very encouraged about your progress until you can work those averages, on the whole, well up into the teens.

I've also put together some questions whose answers should give you an even better idea of how to evaluate yourself. To take the test, jot down the number of each question on a piece of paper and beside it mark which of the following letters most closely describes what you think your performance would be in the situation mentioned in the question:

A. Almost always
B. Most of the time
C. About half the time
D. Less than half the time
E. Hardly ever

Your Ground Game

1. In a typical baseline rally, do your forehand drives land beyond the service line of your opponent? (Note: Answer as indicated above as, for example: "B" if they land beyond the service line "most of the time," "C" if they land there about half of the time," etcetera.)

2. How about your backhand drives under the same conditions?

3. If a ball is hit reasonably deep and in the

middle of your court, but you have time to set up for the shot, can you hit your forehand return equally well crosscourt, down the line, or in the center? In other words, in whatever direction you want?

4. How about a backhand return under the conditions described in Question 3?

5. When you have to run more than a few steps to get to a ball, can you return from the forehand side with consistency?

6. How about a backhand when you have to run for it?

7. Your opponent has come to the net behind a fairly deep approach shot. You have time to set up. Can you execute a successful down-the-line forehand passing shot?

8. The same situation as 7, but a crosscourt forehand passing shot?

9. The same situation as 7, but a down-the-line backhand passing shot?

10. The same situation as 7, but a backhand crosscourt passing shot?

11. Can you consistently return a very hard-hit ball, like an excellent first serve, on your forehand side?

12. What about your backhand under the same condition?

13. Your opponent has hit a high bouncing ball deep to your forehand corner. Can you hit it back deep?

14. What about from your backhand corner?

15. Can you hit a top-spin forehand when you want to?

16. How about a top-spin backhand?

17. Can you slice your forehand and still control the shot?

18. Can you hit your backhand with underspin?

19. A ball is bouncing soft and high near the service line. Can you put it away with your forehand?

20. What about the same shot off your backhand?

21. Can you take pace off your forehand and not lose control?

22. How about your backhand?

23. If you were trading forehands in a rally with most of the people you usually play against, do you figure your opponent would make the first error?

24. How about trading backhands?

25. Your opponent has hit a ball that bounces on the service line. He is two feet behind the baseline. The time is ripe for a dropshot. Can you successfully hit it with your forehand?

26. How about your backhand?

27. Do your forehand lobs usually land *behind* the service line?

28. How about your backhand lobs?

29. Can you use your forehand lob as an offensive weapon—to win points with it?

30. Can you use the backhand lob as an offensive weapon?

31. When the situation calls for it, can you execute a successful forehand top-spin lob?

32. How about a backhand top-spin lob? (Be honest, now!)

33. Can you hit short angled drop shots off your forehand?

34. How about your backhand?

35. You've just pulled your opponent well out of position with a wide serve. The return bounces shallow in the middle of the court. Can you put the next shot away off your forehand?

36. How about your backhand?

37. In a typical set will you hit as many as three or four winners off forehands hit on the run?

38. What about backhands on the run?

Your Net Game

39. When a return is hit short, do you try to get to the net?

40. When you're at net against most of the people you play, do you feel confident that you'll win the point?

41. Do your forehand volleys generally land beyond the service line when you want them to?

42. How about your backhand volleys?

43. Can you place your forehand volley to either side of the court with equal consistency?

44. Your backhand volley?

45. You're at the net and a ball is hit high to your forehand side. How often will you hit a winner?

46. What about the high backhand?

47. How often can you get back a forehand volley when the ball has dipped below the top of the net?

48. How about a low backhand volley?

49. Can you hit a successful stop forehand volley?

50. How about a stop backhand volley?

51. When you get the chance, do you poach in doubles?

52. How often do you win the point when you do poach?

53. You're in position to hit a medium high, medium deep overhead. How often do you figure to win the point?

54. Can you place the overhead in either the deuce or ad court?

55. If you were playing against someone who had your overhead, would you choose to lob against him much?

56. When a ball bounces at your feet, how often can you scoop up the half volley on the forehand side?

57. How about the backhand side?

58. If you were playing somebody with your net game, would you try to keep him or her in the backcourt as much as possible?

Your Serve

59. Do you get your first serve in at least seventy-five percent of the time?

60. Do you average *less* than three double faults per set?

61. Can you hit the ball toward either corner of the service box and still feel confident that the ball will go in?

62. Can you hit a slice serve wide to your opponent's forehand?

63. If you were playing somebody with *your* second serve, would you move in several steps and try to put the ball away?

64. Against an average opponent, do you figure to hit at least two aces per set?

65. Do you invariably spin your second serve?

66. The score is 4–4 in the nine-point tie breaker, and you are serving against your typical opponent. How often do you figure you'll win the set?

Your Return of Serve

67. Do you return as successfully from the backhand side as you do from the forehand side?

68. If you were serving against someone who had your return of service, would you ease up on the first serve so you wouldn't have to deal with a forcing return off your second serve?

69. Can you successfully hit back your forehand returns at a sharp angle?

70. How about backhand returns?

71. The best way to cope with a good server and volleyer is to return the ball low and at his feet. Can you do it off your forehand?

72. How about your backhand?

73. Do you generally move up to hit offensive shots off of second serves?

74. If you were playing doubles with any one of your regular partners at random and you had

to pick one of you to receive service on the final point of the tie breaker, would you pick yourself?

Your Game in General

75. You're ahead in games 5–4 against a player who plays at about your level. It's your serve. How often do you figure to win the set?

76. What if you're behind in the same circumstances?

77. If you're losing in a match, can you switch tactics to throw your opponent off his rhythm?

78. Are you able to overcome factors like wind or sun?

79. If you were the coach of a team consisting of you and most of the players *at your level,* how often would you pick yourself to play a pressure match?

80. Do you play your best under pressure?

Analyzing Your Score

To figure out your score on the preceding test is simple. Give yourself 5 points for every A answer; for every B answer give yourself 4; for every C answer 3; for every D, 2, and don't credit yourself with anything if you have to answer E.

Now add up all your points together and rate as follows:

350–400: Level V
301–349: Level IV
201–300: Level III
101–200: Level II
000–100: Level I